Cambridge E

M000019552

Elements in Religion and Monotheism
edited by
Paul K. Moser
Loyola University Chicago
Chad Meister
Bethel University

MONOTHEISM, BIBLICAL TRADITIONS, AND RACE RELATIONS

Yung Suk Kim
Virginia Union University

CAMBRIDGE
UNIVERSITY PRESS

CAMBRIDGE
UNIVERSITY PRESS

University Printing House, Cambridge CB2 8BS, United Kingdom

One Liberty Plaza, 20th Floor, New York, NY 10006, USA

477 Williamstown Road, Port Melbourne, VIC 3207, Australia

314–321, 3rd Floor, Plot 3, Splendor Forum, Jasola District Centre, New Delhi – 110025, India

103 Penang Road, #05–06/07, Visioncrest Commercial, Singapore 238467

Cambridge University Press is part of the University of Cambridge.

It furthers the University's mission by disseminating knowledge in the pursuit of education, learning, and research at the highest international levels of excellence.

www.cambridge.org
Information on this title: www.cambridge.org/9781108984805
DOI: 10.1017/9781108985383

First published 2022

A catalogue record for this publication is available from the British Library.

ISBN 978-1-108-98480-5 Paperback
ISSN 2631-3014 (online)
ISSN 2631-3006 (print)

Monotheism, Biblical Traditions, and Race Relations

Elements in Religion and Monotheism

DOI: 10.1017/9781108985383
First published online: February 2022

Yung Suk Kim
Virginia Union University

Author for correspondence: Yung Suk Kim, yungsuk@gmail.com

Abstract: In the Hebrew Bible, various aspects of theism exist though monotheistic faith stands out, and the New Testament largely continues with Jewish monotheism. This Element examines diverse aspects of monotheism in the Hebrew Bible and their implications to others or race relations. Also, it investigates monotheistic faith in the New Testament writings and its impact on race relations, including the work of Jesus and Paul's apostolic mission. While inclusive monotheism fosters race relations, exclusive monotheism harms race relations. This Element also engages contemporary biblical interpretations about the Bible, monotheistic faith, and race/ethnicity.

Keywords: Monotheism, Bible, race relations, Hebrew Bible, New Testament

ISBNs: 9781108984805 (PB), 9781108985383 (OC)
ISSNs: 2631-3014 (online), 2631-3006 (print)

Contents

1 Introduction

Race relations are an increasingly important topic – more now than ever before. Racism is not merely a lack of love or a deficiency of intellect, but it is a cancerous evil. On the one hand, there are myths about race or "others," and on the other, there are prejudices and animosity against different races and cultures. People often categorize others, based on race or ethnicity, and rank them by their intellect or culture. Racism begins with a notion that human races are discernibly distinct or differentiated and that some races are superior to others. But this notion is an illusion because dividing lines between races are ambiguous or unscientific.[1] Excellence in human capacity or virtue is widespread among different races or cultures. What constitutes excellence in humans or culture is a matter of debate. No single standard or factor can determine a person or culture's excellence.

Humans have existed for a long time and maintained diverse cultures, living in many regions of the world. So, naturally, their looks and culture have been differentiated, but these differences should not overthrow the singularity of humans who share more similarities than differences. Given the common humanity of *homo sapiens*, while we look different and think differently, we can seek the common causes of justice, peace, and prosperity. In the story of Genesis, God blesses humans and invites them to be fruitful and to multiply so that they may live fully in wider, different places.[2] God's design for humanity is diversity, not homogeneity. Against God's wish, as the episode of the Tower of Babel shows (Gen 11:1–9), people did not scatter but gathered to make a big city, speaking one language. This episode sheds new light on how people must think about race or ethnicity. That is, race, ethnicity, or culture should not be a hiding place or a haven where people stay together among themselves only without engaging others. Race or culture matters not because it is the source of identity or pride but because it is an expression of diversity in God's creation. Like a flowing stream or river, race or ethnicity must be the concept of flexibility that engages otherness and other people. In doing so, people in any culture or ethnicity may learn from others. Since no humans are perfect, they need to help one another, learning from others, while maintaining both the singularity of human character and the diversity of culture.

To address and improve race relations, we will examine monotheism in biblical traditions, which includes both robust insights for race relations and deleterious effects on them. While the former comes from ethical monotheism that helps foster race relations, the latter comes from exclusive monotheism that

---

[1] Sussman, *The Myth of Race.*
[2] Hiebert, "The Tower of Babel and the Origin of the World's Cultures," pp. 29–58.

harms others. What is worse, many interpreters have read some biblical texts, such as John's Gospel or Matthew's Gospel, from the perspective of a triumphant gospel that conquers other cultures. Nevertheless, ethical monotheism with inclusive faith helps improve race relations.

1.1 Why This Element

The Bible does not present a single view of God or theology and includes divergent aspects of monotheism. On the one hand, there is exclusive monotheism that harms other people, as in the story of Joshua's conquest of the Canaanites. This exclusive monotheism, coupled with the notion of "chosenness," leads to the suppression of other people and cultures. Could God be pleased if the Canaanites were annihilated? Should Israelites be happy with seeing the demise of the Canaanites? Here, we see the limitation of monotheism that hinders other people from encountering the truth of God. On the other hand, ethical monotheism is conducive to good race relations. God is inclusive of all, calling for mercy, love, and justice for all. The divine mandate is simple. As God is holy, his people must seek holiness and love others as themselves (Lev 19:18; Matt 5:43–48; Rom 13:8–10; Gal 5:14). But even with ethical monotheism, if people do not follow the ethical teachings of God, there would be no racial equality or diversity.

While race relations seemed to improve for some time, we have not yet seen radical improvement. Racism abounds in society as well as in the minds of people. It is not limited to the so-called developed world such as the USA or European countries. Racism is also prevalent in other developing countries to which cheap labor is brought from the poorest countries. Worse, the fast-growing global economy and forced migrations due to war or natural disasters make race relations complex. Still worse, the global virtual environment has presented Janus-faced aspects of race relations. It provides a free hospitable online space through which people may better understand each other. But at the same time, it may serve as a vehicle of disinformation, becoming a hotbed of prejudice or hatred against others. Given these realities, the topic of race relations is more important than ever before, and we need to improve them not only by reinterpreting monotheism in biblical traditions but also by exploring the way we engage with others and reimagine our relationship with God and our neighbors.

1.2 Key Terms

This Element employs a few important technical terms and concepts that need to be explained and clarified from the outset.

1.2.1 Polytheism

Polytheism is a belief that there are many gods and that people worship them freely. It is believed that ancient Israelites, like other ancient people, had such a view.[3] The Hebrew Bible acknowledges "many heavenly creatures, calling them 'gods' (Gen 6:2; Ps 29:1; 82:6; 86:8; 89:7; Job 1:6), 'angels' (Num 20:16; 2 Sam 24:16; 1 Kgs 13:18; Zech 1:11–12; Ps 78:49; Job 33:23), and 'the assembly of holy ones' (Ps 89:5)."[4] Glimpses of this polytheistic view are also in different biblical traditions: Yahwistic, Elohist, Deuteronomistic, and Priestly. While Yahwistic and Elohist traditions derive from different names of God, Deuteronomistic and Priestly writers reinterpreted the preexisting biblical traditions and had their peculiar views of God.

1.2.2 Henotheism

Henotheism means devoted worship of one god among other gods. When David unified different tribes in Palestine into a single state, he banned people from worshipping other gods, allowing Yahweh alone to be worshipped. He also made Jerusalem the center of Yahwistic cultic activities. In this way, David solidified his power and dynasty. Centuries later, Josiah perfected the removal of other gods through his religious reforms (2 Kgs 22–23). The Ten Commandments also preserve relics of henotheism since what is required is Yahweh-alone worship among other gods. Psalm 95:3 also hints at the existence of other gods: "For the Lord is a great God, and a great King above all gods." Similarly, Psalm 82:1 also says: "God has taken his place in the divine council; in the midst of the gods he holds judgment."

1.2.3 Monotheism

Monotheism is a belief that there is only one God. This view of God is observed in the Priestly creation story (Gen 1:1–2:3) and postexilic writings such as Ezra and Nehemiah, which reflect Jewish exiles' experience after the Babylonian captivity. Out of their painful experience in exile, Priestly writers interpreted the exilic experience as God's punishment and ensured their absolute loyalty to one God.[5] This punishment was due to sin and going after other gods of Canaan, which had been forbidden. The Shema (Deut 6:4) also expresses monotheistic faith.

---

[3] Sommer, *The Bodies of God and the World of Ancient Israel*, pp. 38–57.

[4] Sommer, "Monotheism in the Hebrew Bible." See also Smith, *The Origins of Biblical Monotheism*, pp. 27–82.

[5] Gnuse, *No Other Gods*, pp. 16, 141–142. See also Smith, *The Origins of Biblical Monotheism*, pp. 135–194. See also Anderson, *Monotheism and Yahweh's Appropriation of Baal*, pp. 23–122.

1.2.4 Ethical Monotheism

Ethical monotheism includes moral exhortations that humans are one and that God cares for them. For example, in the Psalms, there is an idea that God is sovereign, cares for the marginalized, and rules people on earth with righteousness (cf, Ps 8; 13; 33; 98). In the covenant code (Exod 20–23), there are humanitarian laws that protect the marginalized although the same laws do not thoroughly satisfy them since, for example, the conditions of slaves remain the same.

1.2.5 Exclusive Monotheism

Biblical narratives also include harsh aspects of monotheism that treat others as enemies. The typical example of this exclusive monotheism is found in the conquest narrative in Joshua. The narrative of liberation in Exodus shifts to a narrative of invasion and killing of Canaanites just because they are non-Israelites or non-covenanted people.

1.2.6 Race, Ethnicity, and Race Relations

In contemporary discussion, generally, while race refers to the physical characteristics of a group, ethnicity focuses on the broad cultural differences of a group. In this Element, these two terms are not distinguished and are used interchangeably since the Element's concern is to explore how (mono)theism affects other people in various historical, social contexts. In this effort, what is required is not race or ethnicity-specific ramifications of monotheism but a broad understanding of how one relates to others, neighbors, aliens, and enemies regardless of race. Race relations apply to this endeavor and depend on multiple conditions besides monotheism. Therefore, this Element deals not only with monotheism but also with related human behavior, ideology, and sociopolitical conditions.

1.3 Outline

We will examine monotheism in the Hebrew Bible and explore its ramifications on race relations. Monotheism is an advanced human thought that seeks universal value for all people. It counters the polytheism of the ancient world, envisions the rule of one God, and promotes the morality of universal value. But the question is: "Do we see this good monotheism in the Hebrew Bible?" The answer is mixed.

In Jewish tradition, monotheism is understood as a historical, theological development over time. The most rigid form of monotheism appears during postexilic times (sixth to fourth centuries BCE). Because of exclusive monotheism, as in Joshua's conquest narrative, Israelites subjugate "others" in the name of one God who gives the land and orders them to kill the Canaanites. This aspect of exclusive monotheism is intensified during postexilic times when Ezra and Nehemiah ask Jews to expel foreign wives and their children. But the Book of Ruth offers a counternarrative to that postexilic, exclusive perspective and legitimizes Ruth, a Moabite woman, who becomes the exemplary "other" to Jews when usually "others" are excluded.

However, in the Hebrew Bible, there is also ethical monotheism that fosters race relations in ways that God rules the world with justice and peace, creates humanity in the image of God, and blesses them to be fruitful and multiply. As in the Tower of Babel narrative in Gen 11:1–9, God wants not univocity among people in one place but the diversity of culture, language, and people in dispersion. Also, in biblical law codes and prophetic traditions, God protects the rights of the marginalized, including resident aliens.

We will also examine monotheism in the New Testament and its ramification on race relations. In the New Testament, Jesus embraces monotheism and promotes ethical monotheism (Matt 5:43–48). Unlike his fellow Jews, he argues that people should love even their enemy. God is impartial to all, the good and the evil. He also overcomes the Jewish definition of neighbor as he tells the parable of the Samaritan (Luke 10:25–37). He changes his mind toward a Canaanite woman who seeks the healing of her daughter because of her persistent, challenging faith that gentiles also deserve blessings from God.

The canonical Gospels also embrace monotheism and argue that Jesus is the Son of God, who was obedient to the will of God. In Matthew's Gospel, Jesus came to fulfill the scriptures and the righteousness of God. The Matthean Jesus, reflecting Matthew's community, struggles to include gentiles in his work but opens the door to everyone (Matt 28:16–20). In John's Gospel, Jesus also believes in one God and confesses that God sent him. He never says that he is God. Rather, he says that God is greater than he (John 14:28). The Johannine Jesus never presents exclusive monotheism, as opposed to a common understanding of John 14:6 ("I am the way, and the truth, . . . no one comes to the Father except through me"). This verse is usually treated as an exclusive theological statement. But it leaves room for engaging others through love and truth. Namely, Jesus's point is that he shows the way of God and testifies to the truth of God. Understood this way, John's Gospel is not the triumphant gospel that conquers other cultures and people.

There are conflicting views about Paul. Some argue that Paul's monotheism is not helpful to race relations because his view of community is rigid and hierarchical. They argue that Paul embraces the Hellenistic ideal of unity (concord) that does not allow for true diversity. But an alternative reading places him as an egalitarian, transformative monotheist. His monotheism is ethical, transformative, and universal and helps foster positive race relations. His mission strategy is to embrace "others" as they are and incorporate them into the household of God. He does not require that gentiles become Jewish (Gal 2:1–11). Paul affirms that God is the God of all, Jews and gentiles (Rom 3:30).

But we should not forget that New Testament texts also have been read narrowly with a focus on exclusive monotheism or Christocentric monotheism in that Jesus is the Lord and God. The claim is he is the only way and the truth, and no other people are saved other than through Jesus who provided salvific knowledge. Otherwise, Jesus's work of God and his faithfulness are rarely discussed. Some people even read some texts from a theology of predestination (or even double predestination) that God destined some for salvation (Eph 1:3–14) and others for damnation.

In the end, the interpreter's job is not to simply take what is stated in the text but to consider how to interpret the text, being aware of what is silenced or ignored in it. On the one hand, as in the case of Joshua's conquest narrative, we can point out the problem of exclusive monotheism and the human ideology of chosenness. But on the other hand, the issue is not the text itself but the exclusivist interpretation that people read into it. Such a case is found in the previously mentioned verse, John 14:6. Is John's Gospel a triumphant gospel or inclusive of others?

2 Theism and Race Relations in the Hebrew Bible

2.1 Polytheism

Polytheism is a belief that there are many gods and that people worship them freely, and it underlies some biblical narratives in the Hebrew Bible at least until the Davidic kingdom was established. Back then in Palestine, there were different tribes that believed in different deities. Ancient Israelites, like other ancient people in the East and West, had many gods and worshipped them. Before David, tribal leaders wished their people to have allegiance to a particular deity, but it was not mandatory. At that time, the focus was to forge strong internal bonds within the tribe or state. Otherwise, there was no room to think of race relations or other people.

2.2 Henotheism

Henotheism emerged during the Davidic kingdom that prohibited its people from worshipping other gods at other places. The only deity that must be worshipped is Yahweh, and the only cultic center is Jerusalem. Henotheism is an expression of both stalwart royal ideology that warrants the Davidic dynasty and the superiority of Yahwism (2 Sam 7), which includes moral teachings about others. As such, David is idealized and spiritualized through subsequent stories about him. David was a musician and poet in his early career, and all the Psalms were associated with him. In many Psalms, there are ideas about God's care for the universe.

2.3 The Historical Development of Monotheism

Monotheistic thinking or philosophy believes that the ultimate or reason governs all people and the world. Historically speaking, it is an advanced human thought that seeks universal value for all. This monotheistic thinking emerged approximately in the sixth century BCE in both the East and the West: Judaism; Greek philosophy with Socrates and Plato; Stoicism in the Hellenistic world; and Eastern religions of Buddhism, Daoism, and Confucianism.[6] With this advanced thought, people can look beyond themselves and be united with others. They may seek the morality of well-being, overcoming blind loyalty to a particular group or state. At the same time, the idealism of oneness may become the ideology for controlling others and other countries.

The idea of monotheism goes back to the time of the pharaoh Akhenaten (1352–1336 BCE), who worshipped the one god, Aten (sun god), prohibiting the worship of other gods. But after him, polytheism flourished again and became the normative worldview.[7] Ancient Israelites also accepted polytheism, as is observed in the Hebrew Bible. The prohibition of other gods in the Ten Commandments supports this view that ancient Israelites were polytheistic. Before David unified the tribes in Palestine and prohibited the worship of gods other than Yahweh, people had worshipped different gods and erected shrines in diverse places. After the unification of the tribes, David became the king of Israel and prohibited the worship of other gods. With the monotheism of Yahweh, David solidified his monarchy and legitimated his kingship by connecting God's covenant with Abraham although he came from a polytheistic environment. However, the most rigid form of monotheism comes after the Babylonian captivity. The Jews who returned from the painful experience of the Babylonian exile reflected on their tragic past and intensified their monotheism, rebuilding the temple, stressing the observance of the law, and cleansing the land by expelling foreign elements. This was also the beginning of rabbinic Judaism, which promoted the monotheistic ideal.

---

[6] Barnes, *In the Presence of Mystery*, pp. 45–66.
[7] Collins, *A Short Introduction to the Hebrew Bible*, p. 25.

2.4 Inclusive Monotheism and Race Relations

Ethical, inclusive monotheism in the Hebrew Bible is the view that there is only one good God who is almighty and loving for all. This view of God is conducive to harmonious human relationships. In the following, we will note positive aspects of ethical monotheism from creation stories, the episode of the Tower of Babel, God's call of Abraham, biblical law codes, and the character of God.

2.4.1 Creation Stories

The creation account in Genesis 1 declares that God Almighty is responsible for the creation of the heavens and the earth. After each day of creation, God said it was good. It is good not because the world is permanent without decay or illness but because it is a viable place to live if people follow the rule of God, who created humankind in his image (Gen 1:28). This implies God's power, freedom, and love, as seen in the creation account and throughout the Hebrew Bible. God wants his creation to exist and prosper abundantly and in good order. In this creation, humans are a special creation because they are created in the image of God and given the right and responsibility to care for the world. They also have the power to decide and communicate with him.[8]

The lofty image of human creation is the view of the priestly class, which is the final redactor of the Torah. According to the Documentary Hypothesis, the creation account in Gen 1:1–2:4a belongs to the Priestly document (P) that views humanity as precious in the image of God.[9] But in Gen 2:4b-24, there is another creation story, which belongs to the Yahwistic document (J) that the Lord God formed the human "from the dust of the ground, and breathed into his nostrils the breath of life" (Gen 2:7). But even here in J's account, humans are more than other creations because God gives "the breath of life" to Adam.

From the creation accounts, we learn that it is one almighty, good God who made all this creation and did so for a purpose, that is, the coexistence of humans with other creatures and nature. Humans must take care of God's creation; they do not have a right to control or exploit it. Nature, animals, plants, all things on the earth are under the care of humans, who are the image of God. After creating all things and humans in his image, God rests on the seventh day, the day that humanity needs to remember his creation and his purpose.

From the creation accounts, we also learn that there are a few important implications for race relations. There is a declaration that once upon a time, God

---

[8] Stanley, *The Hebrew Bible*, pp. 171–179.
[9] For a summary of the Documentary Hypothesis, see Coogan, *A Brief Introduction to the Old Testament*, pp. 44–48.

created the heavens and the earth and reordered the chaotic, dark world.[10] God
spoke and (re)created or reordered the existent chaos, creating humans in his
image to have communication with them.[11] This important beginning is the
beginning of a new humanity that recognizes the notion of one God and one
human family. One noble God created humans in his image and gave them the
task of caring for his creation. As a family of God, they must love one another.
Race relations need this notion that once upon a time, there was one start, one
God, one love, and one human race.

2.4.2 The Tower of Babel

God's will to humans is clear that they must be fruitful and multiply. God wants
them to live in wider regions on earth, with prosperity and diversity. The episode
of the Tower of Babel (Gen 11:1–9) is a violation of God's design for the world
and humanity. People wanted to stay in a city and to build a tower, a symbol of
human pride and civilization. The problem is not that they erect the high-rise
tower but that they do not want to scatter on earth, fearing their uncertain future.
The divine command was to fill the earth (Gen 1:28; 9:1), but the problem was
people did not keep that command and tried to live by and for themselves, being
"isolated from the rest of the world."[12] When people gather in one place, build
their lives within that bound, and speak only one language, new problems arise
and abound. First, there will be new elites or leaders who will emerge, controlling ordinary people with the ideology of unity. The consequences will be
inequalities and injustices in society. Second, people are either brainwashed
by the leaders or forced to follow the norm of a hierarchical unity. Then there
will be no diversity in the community or society. Third, this rigidly unitary
society confronts others and treats them as enemies. There will be no good,
mutual relationship between them, let alone learning from each other. There
might be a culture of hatred and competition against others in different cultures.

But God calls for a diversity of thoughts and cultures and the fruitfulness of
humans. Humanity's prosperity is possible when they are in tension with other
people and other cultures. If a stream does not flow, it will dry and decay. Even
one strong flourishing culture needs new exposure to different cultures. Both

---

[10] In Gen 1:1, the Hebrew word *bereshit* is a combined noun with the preposition "in" and does not
include the definite article in it. So the meaning of this word is "in a beginning," that is, "in the
beginning of God's creation." Coogan, *A Brief Introduction to the Old Testament*, p. 28. This
beginning is not the beginning of history. So the New Revised Standard Version translates Gen
1:1 as "In the beginning when God created . . . ." This translation means that once upon a time
God created the heavens and earth.

[11] Birch et al., *A Theological Introduction to the Old Testament*, p. 43.

[12] Birch et al., *A Theological Introduction to the Old Testament*, p. 58.

leaders and ordinary people need to see what other states and people are doing and learn lessons from them so that they may continue to prosper.

2.4.3 God's Call of Abraham

There is also inclusive, ethical monotheism in the story of Abraham, especially in Gen 12:1–3. He is called out of nowhere and blessed to be the source of blessings for all people on earth (Gen 12:1–3; 15:1–21).[13] He is from the ancient city called Ur of the Chaldeans, and the text does not say that he did something great to deserve God's call. But by the grace of God, he got a chance to start a new journey of faith and hope, becoming the father of many nations including Israel. The sovereign God says to Abraham: "Go from your country and your kindred and your father's house to the land that I will show you" (Gen 12:1). Abraham obeys this call of God and becomes a pioneer to the new world of possibilities.[14] He takes a drastic, radical departure from his comfort zone and moves to the unknown, bleak future with hope. His departure is contrasted with the story of the Tower of Babel where people want to build a great city. He becomes the beacon of hope for all who are nobodies, those who are hopeless and lost such as wandering migrants, refugees, and the poor. God's grace does not fall short of calling and blessing people like Abraham. His name means the father of many nations (Gen 17:5), not merely the beginning of Jews or Israel, though the Yahwist epic puts Israel at the center of the world.

Although Jews claim Abraham as their sole founding father and his call as the beginning of their state, the call story of Abraham is open to interpretation in that the point is not to establish Israel but to start new humanity through Abraham and his faith. He is a paragon of faith for all people coming after him. Paul also considers Abraham the archetype of faith, and God promised the good news to all people who are coming through faith (Gal 3:8).

In sum, God is gracious and sovereign, calling his people to depart from a comfort zone or the place of hopelessness. Not any humans or any institution can be a sole power that overwrites God's grace or power. All need God's grace and directions, seeking a life of diversity. While monoculture or the sense of unity may be necessary for group identity or formation, it may become an obstacle to diversity and dialogue with other cultures. Encountering different people and cultures may be a challenge on one's journey, but it is a space for growth and transformation. It may take place at the borderlands where people find common ground amid differences or disputes. That common ground may be the realization that they are all weak and that they need God's grace. With this realization, they may seek mutual solidarity rather than mutual competition.

---

[13] Von Rad, *Genesis*, pp. 159–160.   [14] Muilenburg, "Abraham and the Nations," pp. 387–398.

I think God's call to Abraham could have been extended to any individual, for there is no special reason or qualification for his call. The fact that he is called to be the father of many nations extends his call beyond Israel to any human nation. Such is the universality of his call.

2.4.4 Law Codes

The Mosaic law has a twofold emphasis: the love of God and the love of neighbor. The former is stated well in Deut 6:4–5, which is called the Shema: "Hear, O Israel: The Lord is our God, the Lord alone. You shall love the Lord your God with all your heart, and with all your soul, and with all your might." As God makes a covenant with Abraham and loves his descendants, they must trust the Lord alone and live by faith. The monotheistic God demands a singular devotion of mind and heart to him. In other words, humanity can be hopeful only in God, and they must put their loyalty only in him. The latter emphasis of love is the love of a neighbor, as in Lev 19:18: "You shall not take vengeance or bear a grudge against any of your people, but you shall love your neighbor as yourself: I am the Lord." When they say they love God, they also must love their neighbors, especially the poor and the marginalized within their community.[15] However, this double command of love does not mean that Israelites can hate non-Jews. Rather, if they love the God of love and covenant, following the example of Abraham and his faithfulness, they must embrace other ethnicities, other religious people, and the marginalized. They must remember God's unconditional call and love to Abraham and rethink their place in God's covenant. God calls Abraham not merely to bless his physical descendants but to bless all the families of the earth (Gen 12:3). That is the theology of the Yahwist.

The covenant code (Exod 21:1–22:16) in the Hebrew Bible affirms the rights of the marginalized, including orphans, the poor, widows, foreigners, and slaves.[16] Deuteronomy 26:5 says, "You shall make this response before the Lord your God: 'A wandering Aramean was my ancestor; he went down into Egypt and lived there as an alien, few in number, and there he became a great nation, mighty and populous'." Biblical covenant codes aim to protect human rights, though they are not perfect compared with today's law codes.[17] They, however, are more protective of the marginalized than the Ancient Near East law codes.[18]

---

[15] Wafawanaka, *Am I Still My Brother's Keeper?* pp. 25–80.

[16] Crüsemann, *The Torah*, pp. 169–200.

[17] Knight, "The Ethics of Human Life in the Hebrew Bible," p. 83.

[18] Kim, "Lex Talionis in Exod 21:22–25," pp. 2–11. See also Evans, "Imagining Justice for the Marginalized," pp. 1–34. See also Van Seters, "Comparison of Babylonian Codes with the Covenant Code and Its Implications for the Study of Hebrew Law."

2.4.5 God's Character and Social Justice

We also see ethical monotheism in the character of God, as observed throughout the Hebrew Bible. First, God hears the cry of Israelites in Egypt and delivers them from the hands of the pharaoh (Exod 2:23–25; 3:7–9). God remembers his covenant with Abraham, takes sides with the oppressed, and frees them from slavery in Egypt. Second, minor prophets such as Amos, Hosea, and Micah emphasize the God of justice.[19] The Lord speaks to his people through Amos:

> I hate, I despise your festivals, and I take no delight in your solemn assemblies. Even though you offer me your burnt offerings and grain offerings, I will not accept them; and the offerings of well-being of your fatted animals I will not look upon. Take away from me the noise of your songs; I will not listen to the melody of your harps. But let justice roll down like waters, and righteousness like an ever-flowing stream (Amos 5:21–24).

Amos harshly criticizes Israelite society and elites who oppress the poor while celebrating their religious festivals, expecting the glory of God in their midst.[20] Justice is the result of what righteousness must be. God is righteous and steadfast; he cares for all, especially for the poor and marginalized. People must follow God's justice and love and make them manifest in every corner of society. Justice is the attribute of "righteous" people; it is social, economic, and restorative justice. All forms of inequalities and injustices must be eradicated, and there must be a fair distribution of wealth and resources. Moreover, less fortunate people, such as the poor or the sick, need time to adjust to society, being given proper care and opportunities.[21] If people follow the character of the righteous God, which is like an ever-flowing stream, there will be waters of justice in a society so that all people will be satiated. Amos's poetic imagination of new society is full of qualities mirroring God's righteousness; they are like a quiet, yet constant, stream of justice in society, like the rolling waters of a river. Here, Amos seems to envision universal justice for all people as God is the God of righteousness and justice.[22] Also note the image of a river flowing indiscriminately in all directions. Wellhausen observes the prophets' moral vision this way: "This is the so-called ethical monotheism of the prophets. They believe in the moral order of the world; they believe in the validity of righteousness as being without exception the supreme law for the whole world. From this point of view, Israel's prerogative now seems to become null and void."[23]

---

[19] Koch, *The Prophets*, pp. 36–62; Hillers, *Micah*, pp. 75–79.

[20] Koch, *The Prophets*, pp. 36–62; Paul, *Amos*, pp. 189–193.

[21] Wafawanaka, *Am I Still My Brother's Keeper?* pp. 25–80.   [22] Koch, *The Prophets*, p. 57.

[23] Wellhausen is quoted in Koch, *The Prophets*, p. 58.

As we have seen previously, the ethical, monotheistic God requires his people to be transformed. The basis of transformation is to imitate the character of God, who is righteous and steadfast. Micah 6:8 condenses what humanity must do to embody God's character: "He has told you, O mortal, what is good; and what does the Lord require of you but to do justice, and to love kindness, and to walk humbly with your God?" The true religion envisioned by the prophet Micah is love-in-action with a humble spirit of God. Likewise, to be transformed, one needs to look at God's holiness, which must be part of everyday life. Lev 19:2 reads: "You shall be holy, for I the Lord your God am holy" (also Lev 20:7, 26; 21:8; Exod 19:6). Holiness is more than religious purification or sanctification; rather, it must be the language of perfection that God wants his people to live by faith, respecting others. If they do so, they are acting in the image of God.

Lastly, in Isaiah and the Psalms, we see the character of the ethical, monotheistic God for all peoples and the whole world. This idea of God is already seen in his covenant with Abraham and through him, God wants all the families of the earth to be blessed (Gen 12:3). Second, Isaiah, witnessing the exile experience in Babylon, thinks of God as the Lord of all. Isa 45:22 reads, "Turn to me and be saved, all the ends of the earth! For I am God, and there is no other." To be saved, people must seek the way of God (Isa 55:6). In Psalm 47:1–2, the kingship over all the earth is very clear: "Clap your hands, all you peoples; shout to God with loud songs of joy. For the Lord, the Most High, is awesome, a great king over all the earth."

2.5 Exclusive Monotheism and Race Relations

Exclusive monotheism is the view that God cares only about a particular, chosen people and that all others are outside of God's love or care.[24] Likewise, God's grace or sovereignty is limited to those who are privileged. This view of monotheism is similar to Christian theologies of predestination and double predestination, which state that God has destined some people for salvation and others for damnation. In the following subsection, we will see some aspects of exclusive monotheism in the Hebrew Bible. There is no question that exclusive monotheism has adverse effects on race relations.

2.5.1 God's Covenant with Abraham

Abraham is the bone of contention for many scholars. He was called out of nowhere. Did God choose him and decide to bless his descendants only,

---

[24] Some scholars pointed out the problem of exclusive monotheism. See Assmann, *Moses, the Egyptian*, pp. 208–218; Assmann, *The Price of Monotheism*, pp. 8–30; Schwartz, *The Curse of Cain*, pp. 15–38; and Kristeva, *Strangers to Ourselves*, pp. 65–76.

excluding all others? If so, God is not an ethical, inclusive God. But as we have seen previously, Gen 12 can be understood as universal, sovereign love that foresees the salvation of all the families of the earth. That is, God called Abraham and blessed him to start a new humanity of hope and blessings through him. The God who called Abraham does not mean to choose only Abraham and to bless his descendants only. That idea is implied in Gen 12:3. Abraham's journey of faith turns the chapter of the dark past and charts a new path filled with hope and promise. In the case of Abraham, God is free to call anyone and does so, not based on merit or origin or any social determinants. We must see God's sovereignty in the act of his calling of Abraham. We need to see this very act of God's calling of Abraham, which must be separate from all the following narratives because the initial account of this story is told and retold, as being interpreted for the reader's interest. In Jewish tradition, Abraham is remembered and told again and again as the founding father of Jews or Israel only, as King David connects his dynasty to Abraham who is promised a great future with multitudes of descendants and land (Gen 15:1–6). What needs to be remembered about God is his unconditional love, grace, and sovereignty. Abraham's faith, also, needs to be highlighted.

Understood this way, there is inclusive, ethical monotheism in this story of Abraham. Therefore, the critical issue is how to understand God's covenant with Abraham and his significance on humanity after him. While Jews consider him as the father of the Jewish state, the very first experience of Abraham as told in Gen 12 is open to interpretation. He is not yet the father of any nation. He even could not have a son because of Sarah's barrenness. As the father of faith, Abraham goes through many trials and tribulations. Even when Isaac is born, God asks Abraham to sacrifice him (Gen 22). In all of these, he shows human weakness, frailty, and even cowardice. Abraham typifies the human struggle on the journey of faith. The point is not that he becomes the father of nations but that his journey for an ideal future is yet to come, needing endurance and trust in God. Nothing has been achieved during his life other than a myriad of trials and possibilities. In the end, my view is that Abraham's initial story does not suggest exclusive monotheism, which claims that God only loves Abraham and his descendants. Abraham could have been anyone, and the manner of his call suggests the universality of his story.

2.5.2 God of Abraham in Gen 16 and Gen 21

As Abraham's story unfolds in Genesis, we see a clear case of exclusive monotheism in the story of Sarah and Hagar (Gen 16; 21). God is on the side of Sarah and Abraham even when they wronged Hagar, her Egyptian slave girl, and Ishmael, the son born from her. Ensuing conflicts between them reveal the harshness of Sarah and Abraham. All this happens because God approved the expulsion of Hagar and his son Ishmael. This is the ugliest story that embeds the seed of conflict between races and classes.

In Gen 16, Sarah initially says to Abraham, "You see that the Lord has prevented me from bearing children; go in to my slave-girl; it may be that I shall obtain children by her" (Gen 16:2). Abraham agreed to that idea. After ten years in the land of Canaan, Sarah took her Egyptian slave girl to Abraham as a wife. Hagar did not have a decision in the process. That is Sarah's decision after much contemplation. Hagar conceived, and Sarah became jealous of her, saying "she looked on me with contempt" (Gen 16:4). Maybe Sarah felt that way even though Hagar did not have contempt for her. With Abraham's consent, Sarah dealt harshly with her, and Hagar ran away from her (Gen 16:6–7). It was utterly morally wrong that Abraham and Sarah harshly dealt with Hagar, who is a foreign, young, pregnant woman. Even the angel of the Lord asks her to return to Sarah and submit to her, cementing class conflict between matriarch and slave girl.

In Gen 21, we see an even more cruel story about Hagar and Ishmael. After Isaac was born in Abraham's old age, Sarah was so happy and felt God was with her. Seeing her son Isaac playing with the son of Hagar the Egyptian, Sarah asks Abraham to cast out Hagar and Ishmael for fear of losing inheritance (Gen 21:9–10). When Abraham lingers on Sarah's request, even God says to him: "Do not be distressed because of the boy and because of your slave woman; whatever Sarah says to you, do as she tells you, for it is through Isaac that offspring shall be named for you. As for the son of the slave woman, I will make a nation of him also, because he is your offspring" (Gen 21:12–13). This God is unethical and different from the God who called Abraham, who was despondent and frail. This is where we must wonder why the initial story of Abraham in Gen 12 is told here in this way. There is no clue that we can find the same God of Abraham here in Gen 21. Instead, we can say that the narrator of this story tells the story with an interest in Jewish royal ideology in mind (the Davidic monarchy).

In the previously mentioned story of Abraham in Gen 16 and Gen 21, Abraham had to take care of Hagar. As he was a wanderer, a nobody from nowhere, Hagar was in a desperate position that needed hope and salvation. Otherwise, she did not need one day's provision of food and drink in the wilderness, as Abraham gave them to her on her departure day. He did this in a way so that he could save face. As the story goes on, God seems to care for her and her son in the wilderness when they are in danger of death because of thirst (Gen 21:15–21). But this episode in the wilderness also saves the face of God. It does nothing more than that. The cruelty of God that expels Hagar and her son is mixed with the image of saving them in such a dire situation that even humans cannot help them out. Ishmael was saved from death, but he lived in the wilderness. The implication is that he would become the father of other nations, not the true covenantal partners. As Abraham's offspring, Ishmael also transmits the blessing of Abraham to his descendants.

2.5.3 The Conquest Narrative in Joshua

The exclusive interpretation of the Abrahamic covenant extends to the conquest of Canaan and the destruction of the Canaanites, as described in the Book of Joshua. Joshua leads the invasion into that land, based on God's command and promise. All living things in the land are the objects of annihilation. Those who were oppressed in Egypt and liberated from Pharaoh's hand now invade other countries and oppress others. What an irony this is! The God of Israel orders such a conquest and threatens the destruction of all. Then, the questions are: "Is this the same God of Abraham who called Abraham out of nowhere? Is this view of the conquering God representing the later ideology of people or a regime like the Davidic Kingdom who needs to conquer others and establish its kingdom?" If the same God of Abraham is only for Israelites and orders the horrible killing of innocent others, we should not embrace this view of God because such an exclusive God is not helpful to humanity at all. From Joshua's conquest story, I do not see the same God of Abraham; the God of Joshua is different from the true God of the universe. The God who was depicted in the Hebrew Bible needs reevaluation, based on the true character of God.[25] So, very plausibly, later political regimes such as the Davidic Kingdom and Jewish elites working with kings edited the patriarchal story to fit in their political program, which was to forge a strong monotheistic government centered on the worship of Yahweh and its cultic center at Jerusalem. For the legitimacy of the Davidic monarchy, David and his theologians needed strong, monotheistic narratives that supported his kingship.

As we have seen previously, the exclusive monotheism, coupled with the exclusive covenant and unique promise of God, differs from the very early story of Abraham who was called out of nowhere. Moreover, when exclusive monotheism is used by the political regime, the effect is so harsh that all otherness and others are suppressed. The kingdom prospers through war, and people of the conquered land are enslaved. For the Davidic monarchy, the truth is that there is one God, one power, and one dynasty going on forever. This truth is religious and political; it is simple yet imperishable. Anyone who challenges this truth will face dire consequences. The world must agree with Davidic unity, and if so,

---

[25] Warrior, "Canaanites, Cowboys, and Indians," pp. 261–265.

God is on their side. David is not concerned with what God wants for him (as Micah conveys the Lord's wish for people, in Mic 6:8).

2.5.4 Monotheism and Royal Ideology

The historical narrative of the Hebrew Bible is not a pure record of what happened; rather, it has a history of composition or redaction in light of later writers' interpretive agenda or concerns.[26] For example, from the Babylonian exile experience, Jews reflect on the past and reconstruct their national, religious life. In this reconstruction, David is considered the most honorable, powerful king who displayed the splendid power and unity of Israel in the name of Yahweh. During the Persian period when Nehemiah led people to rebuild the wall of Jerusalem, he and his group of people were interested in building their identity based on the picture of the Davidic Kingdom's glory in Jerusalem, not in any other place. They claim that Jerusalem is the only holy, royal place where the temple is a symbol of God's presence and protection. Jerusalem is superior to other cities, and that people need protection from all sorts of peril or foreign threats. This royal ideology demands people's obedience to the high priests, political and religious leaders. As monotheism and royal ideology are combined, ordinary people's suffering becomes intense, and other races/ethnicities are suppressed or demolished through constant wars. This royal ideology derives from a political interest that the Davidic Kingdom should be more blessed and powerful so that people might follow the royal court. Narratives of kings and royal courts are political stories intertwined with religious claims as such, for example, that God ordains only kings, priests, and prophets, all of whom are the upper-class leading people.[27]

Royal ideology also serves as a tool to deal with internal and external pressures in society. Internal ones mainly have to do with heterogeneous social groups, and external ones with the "re-emerging powers to the north and south."[28] The opposition force among the urban elites confronts the royal power. To deal with these matters, the royal power needed ideological support from the people, appealing to religious symbols, religious practices, and religious royal ideology that a king plays the role of a divine agent (or divine in Egypt) as shown in royal psalms (Psalms 45; 89; 101; 110).[29] The Israelite Temple functions at the center of royal ideology, which affirms a king as

---

[26] McNutt, *Reconstructing the Society of Ancient Israel*, p. 5.

[27] Actually, we do not know how ordinary people responded to the royal ideology as such. The historical narrative is one side of a political story without knowing or listening to the other part of the story from ordinary people. See Gottwald, *The Politics of Ancient Israel*, pp. 32–112.

[28] Whitelam, "Israelite Kingship," p. 119.   [29] Whitelam, "Israelite Kingship," p. 132.

a divine choice, and also appeals to the public mind through the symbolic presence of God.[30]

In conclusion, though the context and reality of ancient society differ from culture to culture together with a variety of ways of doing royal ideology, an essential need for royal ideology does not differ: the king as the head of the nation-state must reign as a guarantor of peace and justice while asking for total obedience to the rule of law.[31] In this way, the royal bureaucracy gains the upper hand manipulating the state business and enjoys all power. Especially in chaotic situations like wars in ancient Southwestern Asia, royal ideology can easily drive people to cooperate with the royal court and bureaucracy.[32]

2.5.5 Rigid Monotheism and Postexilic Community

A rigid form of exclusive monotheism is found in the postexilic community in Jerusalem. After the painful exile experience in Babylon, Jewish leaders such as Nehemiah and Ezra attempted to rebuild Jewish life based on the laws and worship experience. To avoid another horrible punishment by God, they built a second temple and tried to revitalize their religious life, teaching and learning God's laws to the extent that all must observe them strictly. Purification laws required them to expel foreign wives and their children. While, in times of crisis or fear, rulemaking is necessary, the postexilic community overacted, becoming a community of surveillance. In such a context, strife and hatred become normal, and love and forgiveness are forgotten. But not all Jews agree to this idea of extreme separation or purification.

The Book of Ruth is a counternarrative to this kind of exclusive monotheism. Ruth, a Moabite woman, becomes a model of an ideal immigrant/foreigner by her choice. She confesses that the God of Jews is a true God and follows Naomi, her mother-in-law back to Judah. But Orpah, the other daughter-in-law, returned to her home. There is nothing wrong with her decision, in fact, that is what the law also allowed. From the perspective of Jews who hear this story of Ruth, she is a model foreigner/minority that can be part of Israel. In some way, she blended with Jewish culture by marrying one of them.[33] But from the perspective of Ruth, we cannot help but imagine her struggle when she moved to Judah. Being surrounded by the unfamiliar hostile environment, she had to endure all hardships because she came by her own choice. As a foreign woman, she was committed to the God of Jews, showing respect to her mother-in-law. Even if

---

[30] De Vaux, *Ancient Israel*, p. 112.

[31] Frankfort, *Kingship and the Gods*, p. 342; McNutt, *Reconstructing the Society of Ancient Israel*, p. 172; De Vaux, *Ancient Israel*, pp. 108–111.

[32] Talmon, *King, Cult and Calendar in Ancient Israel*, p. 67.

[33] Yee, "She Stood in Tears amid the Alien Corn," pp. 119–140.

she was the mother of the baby born from her, the child belongs to Naomi. She was still ethnically a Moabite and could not have her full humanity in the foreign land of Judah.[34]

3 Monotheism and Race Relations in the New Testament

3.1 Monotheism, Jesus, and Race Relations

The historical Jesus was a devout Jew who believed in one God and loved Jewish scriptures.[35] As a Jew, he was an advocate for an ethical, universal God who loves all peoples. In other words, Jesus was an inclusive monotheist whose teaching is radically different from other Jews of his time.[36] While the Pharisees emphasized the strict observance of the law, he had more interest in the universal love of God, who does not discriminate against anyone. So he reinterprets Jewish scripture and says that people must be perfect as God is and that they love even their enemies:

> You have heard that it was said, "You shall love your neighbor and hate your enemy." But I say to you, Love your enemies and pray for those who persecute you, so that you may be children of your Father in heaven; for he makes his sun rise on the evil and on the good, and sends rain on the righteous and on the unrighteous. For if you love those who love you, what reward do you have? Do not even the tax collectors do the same? And if you greet only your brothers and sisters, what more are you doing than others? Do not even the Gentiles do the same? Be perfect, therefore, as your heavenly Father is perfect (Matt 5:43–48).

In his reinterpretation of Jewish scriptures, Jesus cites Lev 19:18 ("love your neighbor as yourself"). In Jewish tradition, this love is understood as caring for fellow Jews, and enemies are not the object of their love. But Jesus takes one bold step and asks people to love their enemies without hating them. In fact, "hating your enemy" is not found in Jewish scriptures, and it may be understood in the context of personal relationships among Jews or in the political context where Jews protest against the horrific killing of innocent people under the harsh rule of the Roman Empire. While we do not know which scripture or which context Jesus refers to, he seems to point out the importance of the ultimate love of God in which all kinds of people are included. Jesus implies

---

[34] Norton, "Silenced Struggles for Survival," pp. 265–279.

[35] Charlesworth, *The Historical Jesus*, pp. 97–121; Kim, *Resurrecting Jesus*, pp. 48–57; Crossan, *The Historical Jesus*, pp. 265–302; Dunn, "Was Jesus a Monotheist?" pp. 104–119. See also Dunn, *Did the First Christians Worship Jesus?* pp. 91–146. Other scholars argue that Jesus was worshipped as God. See Hurtado, *Honoring the Son*, pp. 1–64; Bauckham, *God Crucified*, pp. 40–69; Fletcher-Louis, *Jesus Monotheism*, pp. 3–30.

[36] Smith and Kim, *Toward Decentering the New Testament*, pp. 31–38.

that hating enemies may not be the ultimate solution to human violence or wars. He approaches the realities of the world from a thoroughgoing, moral perspective that people need a fundamental change in their minds and hearts toward God and their neighbors.[37] Jesus asks for a change of mind, which in Greek is *metanoia*, repentance (Mark 1:15). That is, people must seek the way of God, the way of love, the way of mercy, and the way of justice and righteousness.[38] Only then, may they live a new life of the kingdom of God, which is the rule/ reign of God. God's new rule of justice and peace is possible for those who change their mind and heart. The way of Jesus is to engage enemies with love and prayer. Those who follow this teaching and live this way are children of God. In other words, if they do not love enemies, they are not children of God. The reason is God is impartial to all, and Jesus says that God "makes his sun rise on the evil and the good, and sends rain on the righteous and the unrighteous" (Matt 5:45). Jesus continues, "For if you love those who love you, what reward do you have? Do not even the tax collectors do the same? And if you greet only your brothers and sisters, what more are you doing than others? Do not even the Gentiles do the same?" (Matt 5:46–47).

As we have seen previously, in Jesus's view of God, God's love is impartial, and therefore, humanity's job is not to fight or win over others but to engage in the love of God and love even their enemies. The case in point will be the parable of the Good Samaritan (Luke 10:25–37), who is an enemy to Jews, but he helps the apparently Jewish man who is half-dying in harm's way. Jesus signifies that different races or cultures are not a threat or an obstacle but helpful to others.[39] In this parable, the lawyer asks Jesus, "Who is my neighbor?" (Luke 10:29). He knows the answer but wants to test Jesus. Then, Jesus tells the story of a Samaritan man, who is not a Jew but an enemy of Jews. While a Jewish priest and a Levite passed by a Jewish man who was robbed and left half-dying, a nameless, foreign traveler stopped to see what happened and took full care of him. At the end of the story, Jesus asks, "Which of these three, do you think, was a neighbor to the man who fell into the hands of the robbers?" (Luke 10:36). The answer must be clear, as the lawyer says reluctantly, "The one who showed him mercy" (Luke 10:37). Then, Jesus says finally, "Go and do likewise" (Luke 10:37).

Jesus redefines "neighbor" not as an object of love but as the subject of love, asking the lawyer to become a neighbor to those who need help regardless of who they are.[40] Being the subject of love means one is the one who should love and that one should be a neighbor to others. Also, Jesus's point is that "others"

[37] Kim, *Resurrecting Jesus*, pp. 53–56.
[38] Kim, *Truth, Testimony, and Transformation*, pp. 47–66.   [39] Kim, *Jesus's Truth*, pp. 76–79.
[40] Kim, *Jesus's Truth*, pp. 76–79.

are not enemies, but they may become neighbors too, to those in need. Essentially, when people see others, they must ask not who they are, where they are from, or whether they are lovable but what they *need*. This way all become neighbors. There may be boundaries between them, but love crosses those boundaries. Likewise, neighborly love must extend to all, regardless of who they are or what language they speak. Indeed, Jesus thinks of a universal family based on one God in heaven, as he says in Mark 3:33–35: "Who are my mother and my brothers? Here are my mother and my brothers! Whoever does the will of God is my brother and sister and mother" (see also Matt 12:48–50; Luke 8:21).

3.2 Monotheism, Gospels, and Race Relations

In the Synoptic Gospels, Jesus appears as the Son of God, who teaches about the kingdom of God, advocates for the weak and marginalized, and because of that, is crucified.[41] But God vindicates him and raises him from the dead. Though the contents of Jesus's work in each Gospel differ from one another because of the community context, the common denominator is that Jesus is God's son who does the work of God. He is not worshipped as a God but is glorified as the Son of God. In all these gospels, the monotheistic God is ethical and inclusive. Let us examine each Gospel briefly.

In the early stage of his public ministry in the Gospel of Mark, Jesus came to Galilee after John was arrested and delivered his initial sermon, which is about "the good news of God," saying, "The time is fulfilled, and the kingdom of God has come near; repent, and believe in the good news" (Mark 1:15). Jesus did not preach about himself or his rule; rather, the substance of his teaching is "the good news of God," which may be either the good news from or about God.[42] Jesus's point is that God must be at the center of humanity and the world and that God must rule the human heart with justice and love. He declares that now is a new time that the new rule of God must be effective and available for those who come to change their mind and heart, which is *metanoia*. "Repent" in 1:15 is not a penitential confession but rather a radical shift to God's reign. Now is the radical new time that all people are equal and live with justice.[43] Jesus came to serve them, especially the oppressed and marginalized, as he says in Mark 10:45: "For the Son of Man came not to be served but to serve, and to give his life a ransom for many."[44] Ironically, serving others cost him his life. If he served only a few powerful people or a few chosen, he would not have been

---

[41] Powell, *The Gospels*, pp. 57–180; Stanton, *The Gospels and Jesus*, pp. 37–96.

[42] Kim, *Resurrecting Jesus*, pp. 53–56.

[43] Blount, *Go Preach! Mark's Kingdom Message and the Black Church Today*, pp. 82–98.

[44] Dowd and Malbon, "The Significance of Jesus' Death in Mark," pp. 271–297.

opposed or crucified. Jesus understands God as the God of all, who cares for all. This idea of universal love of God is implied in the parable of the Mustard Seed where the seed is sown upon the ground (*ge*), any lot or place in the world.[45] The ground symbolizes the indiscriminate work of God for anyone or any place. In Matthew, the seed is sown on the field (*argos*), a prepared place, while in Luke, it is sown upon the garden (*kepos*), a cultivated yard. In Mark, the emphasis is that God's impartial, radical work of love and justice must be available for anyone in any place. The implication is that race, gender, or ethnicity does not matter to the love of God, while each of these is important.

In Matthew's Gospel, one of the pivotal issues is the mission boundary. That is, should the predominant Jewish Christian community open the good news of God to the gentiles? Then, what might be the condition? Do the gentiles need to keep Jewish laws when they join the Christian community? The climactic event that deals with all these questions appears in Matthew 15:21–28 where the Matthean Jesus reflects the mission context of Matthew. This story reflects the community's struggle to open the mission to the gentiles.[46] Jesus refuses to listen to the Canaanite woman and does so three times only to emphasize his exclusive theology that Jews are the only privileged children of God. His disciples also intervened, saying, "Send her away, for she keeps shouting after us" (Matt 15:23). They reflect the atmosphere of the Matthean community that struggles to open the gospel to the gentiles. Earlier in Matt 10:5, Jesus already told his disciples to not go to the gentiles when they go out for a mission because they are not Jews: "Go nowhere among the Gentiles, and enter no town of the Samaritans." Here again, in Matthew 15:24, Jesus utters a similar word: "I was sent only to the lost sheep of the house of Israel" (Matt 15:24). But the woman was persistent in her request for healing and blessing because she had faith that God is the God of all, and the Messiah for all, not only for Jews. Yet, finally, in Matthew 15:28, Jesus changes his mind and acknowledges her faith: "O woman, great is your faith." This is a radical change for Jesus that he now officially opens his mission to the gentiles. The implication for the Matthean community is that now the community should open the door to other races and ethnicities. The only condition is faith in God, who loves and blesses all. This faith is a common denominator that all people need. Anyone can join the house of God through faith. In the end, Matthew's gospel is inclusive of other races and all people, as Jesus's genealogy includes foreign women. At the end of the Gospel, Jesus commissions his disciples to teach what he taught, which is the love of God. He did not ask them to conquer other religions, cultures, and

---

[45] Kim, *Jesus's Truth*, pp. 24–28.

[46] Schipani, "Transformation in the Borderlands," pp. 13–24; Patte, "The Canaanite Woman and Jesus," pp. 33–53; Guardiola-Sáenz, "Borderless Women and Borderless Texts," pp. 69–81.

people. The great mission is to tell the good news that God cares for all, and his disciples must continue his work of God, ensuring justice in society, feeding the hungry, and welcoming strangers and refugees (Matt 25:31–46).[47]

The Gospel of Luke, unlike Matthew's Gospel, has a gentile audience in mind from the beginning. It is a very universal gospel with the theme of gentile preference, which Jesus preached at his hometown synagogue (Luke 4:16–30).[48] After reading Isaiah 61:1–2: "The Spirit of the Lord is upon me, because he has anointed me to bring good news to the poor. He has sent me to proclaim release to the captives and recovery of sight to the blind, to let the oppressed go free, to proclaim the year of the Lord's favor," Jesus told them, "Today this scripture has been fulfilled in your hearing." Then people were happy because of this well-known scripture Jesus read and thought that they were truly blessed. But to their dismay, Jesus told them God loves the gentiles. His point is that God sent his prophet Elijah to the widow at Zarephath when there were many widows in Israel; likewise, God sent Elisha to the Syrian army general Naaman to cure his leprosy even when there were many lepers in Israel. This Lukan Jesus is the opposite of the Matthean Jesus and says his mission is to seek out and to save the lost (Luke 19:10). The lost people in the Lukan Gospel are primarily those who are considered nobodies, sinners, and social outcasts. They hear the good news of God that Jesus preaches. In his healing and teaching, Jesus redefines "neighbor" in the parable of the Good Samaritan (Luke 10:25–37), saves Zacchaeus the tax collector who repents and restores justice to the people in need, as in the parable of the Rich Man and Lazarus (Luke 16:19–31) and the parable of the Unjust Judge and the Widow (Luke 18:1–8).

In John's Gospel, Jesus also believes in one God and confesses that God sent him. He never says that he is God in this Gospel. As opposed to the traditional view that Jesus is God, which is called "high Christology," a new perspective on the Fourth Gospel presents him as a Jewish Messiah who does the work of God.[49] In this Gospel, his consistent point is that he is sent by God and does his work. He says he is not greater than the one who sent him. His job is to deliver the word of God and embody it. The nucleus of the word of God is the love of God. John 3:16 says, "For God so loved the world that he gave his only Son, so that everyone who believes in him may not perish but may have eternal life." Jesus's task is to embody the word of God so that people may understand and live with it. When he says, "I am the way, and the truth, and the life. No one comes to the Father except through me" (John 14:6), he points out the import- ance of his work of God. That is, he follows the way of God, testifies to the truth

---

[47]   Smith and Kim, *Toward Decentering the New Testament*, pp. 39–44.

[48]   González, *The Story Luke Tells*, pp. 15–76.

[49]   Kim, *Truth, Testimony, and Transformation*, pp. 1–66.

of God, and helps people live in truth. Those who follow Jesus as he does may be accepted by God. In other words, Jesus is not the ladder to heaven; his way of life is the way to God. The implication is that people need to see his finger that points to God. He is not himself the way, but his life that embodies the word or truth of God is. Understood this way, there is no exclusivism in John 14:6; rather, Jesus's saying is an invitation to live like him, delivering the love of God to the world, overcoming hatred and oppositions, and testifying to the truth of God that God loves all and ensures justice for everyone. John's Gospel is not a triumphant gospel that conquers other cultures and invades other countries.

The Johannine community began with painful separation from the synagogue due to its faith that Jesus is the Messiah and struggled to survive as a Jewish Christian community.[50] So, initially, the community has animosity against the synagogue and legitimates itself by arguing that the Jesus-followers are superior to other Jews. With dualistic, ultimatum language, they say they are the only children of God, and other Jews are children of the devil (John 8:39–47). But as time goes by, the Johannine community undergoes a time of transformation and renews itself with an emphasis on God's universal love, Jesus's testimony to the truth of God (not Rome's truth), and the participation by Jesus-followers. In the end, John's Gospel is not an imperial, triumphant gospel that excludes other religions or other cultures but a gospel that invites all people to live like Jesus so that they may live abundantly with God's peace and love (cf, John 3:16).

3.3 Monotheism, Paul, and Race Relations

Paul was a Pharisee and grew up in a Hellenistic environment.[51] He was thoroughly a monotheist. For him, the God of the Hebrew Bible is the true God, and his Son is Jesus. In 1 Thessalonians 1:9–10, one of the earliest letters he wrote, he tells the gentile converts in Thessalonica that God is "a living and true God" and that his Son from heaven will come soon to rescue them "from the wrath that is coming." So he asks the early gentile converts to turn away from idols to God. In Paul's view, Jesus was the Son of God who manifested God's righteousness (Rom 3:21–26).[52] Jesus was faithful to God and humanity and did not spare his life to demonstrate God's love and justice. He was glorified as the Son of God because he was obedient to God. For Paul, Jesus is not the same as God because, on the last day, he "hands over the kingdom to God the Father, after he has destroyed every ruler and every authority and power" (1 Cor 15:24). Once Jesus finishes his work on the last day, "then the Son himself will also be

---

[50] Martyn, *History and Theology in the Fourth Gospel*, pp. 35–66; Culpepper, *The Gospel and Letters of John*, pp. 54–61.

[51] Roetzel, *Paul*, pp. 19–37.

[52] Kim, *Rereading Romans from the Perspective of Paul's Gospel*, pp. 4–105.

subjected to the one who put all things in subjection under him, so that God may be all in all" (1 Cor 15:28). Paul makes it clear that God is everything; God is all in all, and his Son submits to him.

Now the question is whether Paul's monotheism is conducive to race relations. There are two kinds of interpreters of Paul. One group thinks that Paul adopted the dominant ruling philosophy of Stoicism – the ideal of unity and oneness.[53] The other group sees him as a theologian who counters the dominant philosophy of Hellenism.[54] In the former, Paul borrows the ideology of oneness and unity (*homonoia*) from Hellenistic Stoicism and applies it to the Christian community. So the Corinthian body is understood as a hierarchical community that Christ is at the center, apostles are next, and other members come after that (1 Cor 12:12–31). In this unified community, there is no true diversity; all must speak the same thing, which means they all must follow the rule of a hierarchy. The high-ranking members are apostles who can speak for the rest. In this view of the community, "the body of Christ" as a metaphor is read as an organism that stresses unity and control. So "you are the body of Christ" is read as "you are the community or church belonging to Christ." Namely, in this view, the church is Christ's. But in Paul's theology, Jesus is rather the foundation of the church (1 Cor 3:11), and the church belongs to God (1 Cor 1:2; 10:32; 11:22; 15:9; 2 Cor 1:1; Gal 1:13).[55] Moreover, in Paul's theological vocabulary, followers of Jesus are asked to unite with Christ, not merely to be unified within a community.[56] This idea is seen in 1 Cor 6:16–20 where Paul says the Corinthians are God's temple, which is holy, and therefore, they must be united with Christ, following his faith and spirit. He says, "Do you not know that whoever is united to a prostitute becomes one body with her? But anyone united to the Lord becomes one spirit with him" (1 Cor 6:16–17). It seems that Paul is not interested in the language of unity in Stoicism that people are one because they are members of a community, but he is more interested in the realism of how people can become one in Christ. That is, they must be united to him, becoming one spirit with him. By following the footsteps of Christ, they may become one. That is union with Christ.

Now let us see the latter group of interpreters who posit Paul as an egalitarian who embraces equality between genders or between ethnicities. These interpreters base their interpretation on Gal 3:28: "There is no longer Jew or Greek,

---

[53] Mitchell, *Paul's Rhetoric of Reconciliation*; Lee, *Paul, the Stoics, and the Body of Christ*; Neyrey, *Paul in Other Worlds*.

[54] Martin, *The Corinthian Body*, pp. 38–68; Kim, *Christ's Body in Corinth*, pp. 39–95; Borg and Crossan, *The First Paul*, pp. 59–154.

[55] Kim, "Reclaiming Christ's Body (*soma christou*)," pp. 20–29; Kim, *A Theological Introduction to Paul's Letters*, pp. 83–108.

[56] Kim, *How to Read Paul.*, pp. 121–133.

there is no longer slave or free, there is no longer male and female; for all of you are one in Christ Jesus." This statement is a radical one that sets a Christian community apart from society with a rigid hierarchy between genders or between classes. But the question is How do we understand "for all of you are one in Christ Jesus"? Does Paul envision a radical egalitarian community that negates social distinctions between genders and between classes? Or does he conceive of a community in Christ where people are treated equally in a Christly manner, while they are maintaining their social distinctions? It seems that given Paul's interim ethics that the end would come so soon, he adopted the latter option. Then, radical equality is not in view, and people stay where they are, as he says in 1 Cor 7:24: "In whatever condition you were called, brothers and sisters, there remain with God." This does not mean that they should give up on the hope of freedom or that they should obey their masters blindly. However, his position about slavery is a bit ambiguous since he does not explicitly say that slavery is wrong or that they must cut off the chain of slavery themselves. Perhaps that was not his primary concern. Since Paul is not an insurrectionist or an abolitionist, as Jesus is not, given his interim ethics, his best advice to his community is to "remain with God." On another note, however, we must note his view of slavery or community is very different from later epistles (Deutero-Pauline and Pastoral Letters) in which household codes regulate various hier-archical social relationships between parents and children, between spouses, and between masters and slaves. These stringent codes push a strict hierarchy that is the norm in society and the church, and such codes allow the church to become a hierarchical community where slaves must obey their masters as Christ did to God.

In sum, Paul is egalitarian in limited ways because of his interim theology that he did not challenge the system directly and thought that the end would come soon. Because of this interim theology, he was passive in dealing with slavery or social injustices. He focused on his community and people only. But ideologically speaking, his view of God is so radical that he challenges the royal ideology of Rome and its strongholds of hierarchical unity. His radical view of God is condensed in 1 Cor 1:26–30:

> Consider your own call, brothers and sisters: not many of you were wise by human standards, not many were powerful, not many were of noble birth. *But God chose what is foolish in the world to shame the wise; God chose what is weak in the world to shame the strong; God chose what is low and despised in the world, things that are not, to reduce to nothing things that are,* so that no one might boast in the presence of God. He is the source of your life in Christ Jesus, who became for us wisdom from God, and righteousness and sanctifi-cation and redemption. (Italics mine for emphasis)

While Paul does not address social issues, his community is a community of love by God; this community includes the marginalized people ("what is foolish; what is weak; what is low and despised in the world"), who are chosen by God. It is believed that many of the Corinthians are from the lower class and that they are welcomed into the church. In Paul's community, the gentiles are accepted into the church through faith, not based on wealth or social status. In this sense, his community is a miniature of a viable community in Christ where all are taken care of.

In Rom 3:29–30, Paul affirms that God is one and that God is not the God of Jews only or the God of gentiles only. All people are welcomed into the people of God through the same faith (Rom 3:30). Inclusion of the gentiles is not based on the law or circumcision or anything else. Potentially, all people are children of God, and they can join the household of God not through race, ethnicity, power, or culture but through faith, which is to trust God and follow the way of Christ.[57] While the law is holy and perfect (Rom 7:12), it has never become the basis for justification because what comes first is faith that is working through love (Gal 5:6). The law without faith is nothing, as faith without works is dead (Jas 2:26). For Paul, the issue is not because the law is imperfect or impossible to keep but because it is misused or absolutized at the sacrifice of faith. He says, "I can testify that they have a zeal for God, but it is not enlightened."[58] He argues that God "will justify the circumcised on the ground of faith and the uncircumcised through that same faith" (Rom 3:30). This is true to the story of Abraham in Gen 12–15 that Abraham is considered "righteous" because he trusts in God. Because of his faith or trust, he had to walk the faith. Faith is not knowledge but an ongoing trust in God and commitment to him. Through faith, Abraham had hope in God and walked until the end of his life. God recognizes Abraham's faith and his continuous journey of commitment. In Gen 15:6, justification is the language of relationship, not that of a legal court that one's status is changed once and forever. In Jewish tradition or in the Hebrew Bible, the problem for Jews was a lack of faith. If they had true faith, they could keep the law. In Paul's theological reasoning, the law is not the first thing. What comes first is God's call or his grace, and then comes faith. Abraham responds to God's grace or his call through faith. Ideally, if there is enough faith in a person or within the community, the law may be kept well. Faith may inform one that one can keep the law properly. The law was added to Israelite society because people lacked enough faith. The law has a positive function, but it should not replace faith. Nevertheless, Paul asks a rhetorical question and answers it

---

[57] Kim, *Preaching the New Testament Again*, pp. 8–36.

[58] Stendahl, "The Apostle Paul and the Introspective Conscience of the West," pp. 199–215; Sanders, *Paul and Palestinian Judaism*, pp. 511–514.

himself: "Do we then overthrow the law by this faith? By no means! On the contrary, we uphold the law."

Paul's inclusive monotheism is also seen in his understanding of God's covenant with Abraham, which is also extended to the gentiles.[59] He argues that the gospel (good news) was declared beforehand to Abraham, which is the blessing of all the gentiles. Gal 3:8–9 reads: "And the scripture, foreseeing that God would justify the Gentiles by faith, declared the gospel beforehand to Abraham, saying, 'All the Gentiles shall be blessed in you.' For this reason, those who believe are blessed with Abraham who believed." This promise of God to the gentiles was confirmed through Christ Jesus, who was faithful to God and humanity. So Gal 3:26 says, "For in Christ Jesus you are all children of God through faith." All people, regardless of who they are, become children of God through faith, which is to follow Christ Jesus. That is, those who are in Christ Jesus must follow his faithfulness. To become children of God, what people need essentially is not specific knowledge, doctrine, or tradition but faith that is working through love (Gal 5:6). Such people of faith are gathered in a community, and they feel oneness in Christ. Though their gender, race, or social class is different in the community, they share the common faith that trusts the God of all, loves one another, and hopes for complete salvation in the end. This faith-driven community is expressed in Gal 3:28–29: "There is no longer Jew or Greek, there is no longer slave or free, there is no longer male and female; for all of you are one in Christ Jesus. And if you belong to Christ, then you are Abraham's offspring, heirs according to the promise."

Likewise, Paul's inclusive monotheism assumes the universal need for salvation for all humanity. He hopes that God will save Israel and all the gentiles. Certainly, for Paul, the dilemma is that not all people come to faith even if God wants them all to be saved. Nevertheless, Paul does not give up on the hope that God will save all, including Israel, in God's way (Rom 11:26). Even if things are not going in the direction he thought, he still hopes that his wish may be heard, which is the salvation of all. He left room for God's providence about the salvation of all. Otherwise, he never overwrote God's sovereignty as if he knew all things about God. Paul's wish for the salvation of all is expressed in Rom 5:18: "Therefore just as one man's trespass led to condemnation for all, so one man's act of righteousness leads to justification and life for all." Also, Rom 11:32 implies Paul's wish for the salvation of all in the end: "For God has consigned all to disobedience, that he may have mercy on all." But Paul is not a universalist, who thinks all are saved automatically. There must be a human response, which is faith. So he says that God will justify the one who has the

---

[59] Kim, *Rereading Galatians from the Perspective of Paul's Gospel*, pp. 14–95.

faith of Jesus, which means sharing in his faithfulness. Likewise, in 1 Cor 15:22, he says: "For as in Adam all die, so also in Christ shall all be made alive." In his monotheistic thinking, Paul does not judge nonbelieving Jews or other people who do not profess faith yet because the future is in God's hand, and they may come to God at any time through the grace of God. God is not necessarily on Paul's side or our side; rather, Paul and we must stand on God's side, trying to understand his immense grace and truth. So Paul has a doxology in Rom 11:33–36:

> O the depth of the riches and wisdom and knowledge of God! How unsearchable are his judgments and how inscrutable his ways! 'For who has known the mind of the Lord? Or who has been his counselor?' 'Or who has given a gift to him, to receive a gift in return?' For from him and through him and to him are all things. To him be the glory forever. Amen.

What we learn from previously mentioned Paul's doxology is that no Christian can judge anyone or any group of people based on his/her presumption of salvation. No one can judge on behalf of God. God is the final judge and arbiter of wisdom. The task for the followers of Jesus is not to judge others but to manifest God's righteousness through faith, following in the footsteps of Jesus.[60] So, in Galatians, Paul ensures that gentile Christians do not need to follow Jewish ways of life; circumcision or dietary laws are not essential to them. While, for Jews, their laws and customs are important to their life, they are not a must for the gentiles. The gospel that came through Jesus cannot be compromised by anything. As the law is not the gospel, culture is not, either. In other words, gentile Christians can maintain their lifestyle or culture while living according to the manner of the gospel, which is an indispensable thing. Paul's mission strategy is to accept diverse people as they are and to help them live for the gospel as children of God. He expresses himself very well regarding this strategy of the gospel, as in 1 Cor 9:19–23:

> For though I am free with respect to all, I have made myself a slave to all, so that I might win more of them. To the Jews I became as a Jew, in order to win Jews. To those under the law I became as one under the law (though I myself am not under the law) so that I might win those under the law. To those outside the law I became as one outside the law (though I am not free from God's law but am under Christ's law) so that I might win those outside the law. To the weak I became weak, so that I might win the weak. I have become all things to all people, that I might by all means save some. I do it all for the sake of the gospel, so that I may share in its blessings.

---

[60] Stendahl, "Religious Pluralism and the Claim to Uniqueness," pp. 181–183; Kim, "Imitators (Mimetai) in 1 Cor 4:16 and 11:1," pp. 147–170.

In conclusion, Paul's inclusive monotheism needs the faithfulness of Jesus. All people need to follow in his footsteps. Then there will be a new life and salvation. Paul is not ashamed of the gospel because it is "the power of God for salvation to everyone who has faith, to the Jew first and also to the Greek" (Rom 1:16). The gospel is not salvific knowledge or conviction about God but the power of God for salvation. As Jesus testified to the good news of God through faith until dying on the cross, his followers must participate in his life and death that he exemplified the good news of God. Because of Jesus's faithfulness, God's righteousness has been revealed to the world.[61] That is, when people experience what God's love and justice look like, they have a goal of life to spread the good news of God to all through Christ Jesus.

3.4 Exclusive Monotheism and Race Relations

Some texts in the New Testament point to exclusive monotheism and therefore have negative effects on race relations. The typical texts are from Eph 1:3–4: "Blessed be the God and Father of our Lord Jesus Christ, who has blessed us in Christ with every spiritual blessing in the heavenly places, just as he chose us in Christ before the foundation of the world to be holy and blameless before him in love." These texts have been often read from the perspective of a rigid doctrine called "predestination" that God chose to save some. Some people go one step further and propose double predestination that God chose some for salvation and others for damnation. But in fact, the previously mentioned text is not explicit about such doctrines. The point of the scripture may be in the language of confession or thanksgiving in that one expresses God's unconditional grace for oneself. One needs to be reminded of Paul's doxology in Rom 11:33–36. Who can know the depth of God's mind?

In some texts of the New Testament, faith is understood as a set of teaching or knowledge that only those who have this faith are saved and given power in the church and world. This view is pictured in some Pastoral Letters (1 Tim 1:3–5; 4:6; 2 Tim 1:5, 13; Tit 1:13), which are not believed to be written by Paul.[62] While correct knowledge about God or Jesus is important, people can emphasize other things as true, or they may ignore other more important aspects of faith, which is participatory faith as we see from Paul's authentic letters. What they emphasize is "faith in Christ" (Eph 1:15; Col 1:4; 1 Tim 1:13–16, 19; 2 Tim 3:15), which means Christ is the object of faith only. In other words, they do not see or emphasize the faithfulness of Jesus Christ, which requires ongoing participation in him. Rather, they think their salvific knowledge about Jesus is

---

[61] Price, "God's Righteousness Shall Prevail," pp. 259–280.

[62] Kim, *Preaching the New Testament Again*, 8–36.

enough and that their salvation is done. In fact, in Paul's authentic letters, he prefers the formula of *pistis Christou* (e.g., Rom 3:22, 26; Gal 2:16), which is a Greek genitive case. While some translate it as "faith in Christ," many modern translators translate it as "the faithfulness of Christ," in which Christ is the subject of faith.[63] Western missionaries went to Africa and Asia with their "faith in Christ" as knowledge and thought that their salvation was done using faith/knowledge. They were full of confidence and felt they were blessed not only with their gospel but with their western culture and civilization. In this triumphant context, Jesus is considered the cosmic king and lord of all, and all his followers rule the world with him. They are triumphant and bring their gospel to the world, invading other countries, demolishing other cultures. Western missionaries in the nineteenth and twentieth centuries went to their mission countries and engaged in these things. They brought their culture to other countries along with the "western" gospel. This attitude toward the mission and other cultures aligns with some other texts in the New Testament. Two more texts will illustrate this point.

While John's gospel is not triumphant, as we have seen previously, people interpret that gospel as a weapon to invade other countries and conquer other peoples with the gospel. They argue that Jesus is God and that he is the way to salvation and heaven. The way here is only through salvific knowledge about Jesus. John 14:6 is a perfect scripture for them to show this. It reads: "I am the way, and the truth, and the life. No one comes to the Father except through me." But the alternative interpretation does not support this exclusive reading because it sees the work of Jesus from these "I Am" sayings. That is, Jesus is the way because he discerned the way of God and lived with it. Jesus testified to the truth of God and because of that he stood before Pilate and was put to death (John 18:37). The truth of God in John's gospel is the love of God, as in John 3:16: "For God so loved the world that he gave his only Son, so that everyone who believes in him may not perish but may have eternal life." Here, "to believe in him" means to take his teaching and live with it. Otherwise, mere believers are not his disciples, as he says in John 8:31–32: "Then Jesus said to the Jews who had believed in him, 'If you continue in my word, you are truly my disciples; and you will know the truth, and the truth will make you free'." In this way, John's Gospel invites readers across the board to work together in embodying the truth of God. Different people and races may share common interests when they struggle in their communities.

---

[63] Johnson, "Rom 3:21–26 and the Faith of Jesus," pp. 77–90; Hays, "PISTIS and Pauline Christology," pp. 35–60. See also Hays, *The Faith of Jesus Christ*, pp. 119–152.

The other oft-cited exclusive text is Matt 28:16–20 (called the Great Commission) that missionaries interpret as a mandate to infringe any borders, personal or geographical. They go to other countries and peoples with a sure set of salvific knowledge about God and Jesus. In doing so, ironically, they propagate disciples not of Jesus, but instead disciples of western ideologies centered on a biased understanding of human development and civilization.[64] They forget what Jesus taught in the parable of the last judgment (Matt 25:31–46) that God rewards those who care for the marginalized, not those who worship Jesus. Or they ignore Jesus's teaching about God's rule or his righteousness in Matt 6:33: "But strive first for the kingdom of God and his righteousness, and all these things will be given to you as well." What they must seek first is God's radical rule that affects all spheres of human life anywhere and everywhere.

4 Contemporary Biblical Interpretation about Others, Race, and Ethnicity

Contemporary biblical interpretation broadly engages the Bible and its impact on race, ethnicity, or race relations.[65] For a long time, the Bible has been read as a single book with a single view of monotheism, which tends to be exclusive of others and their cultures. But such a view is challenged by many contemporary scholarly perspectives. African American scholars have pointed out the problems of racial interpretation in that Ham is labeled as an ancestor of the Africans and that Hagar becomes a perpetual slave woman and foreigner outside of God's covenant.[66] Likewise, feminist and womanist scholars deconstruct androcentric texts and interpretations that privilege male or elite views, challenging and rejecting all forms of chauvinistic, foundational interpretations of the text.[67] Postcolonial interpretation also challenges all forms of ideology in biblical narratives, including exclusive power relations and truth claims, on the one hand. On the other hand, some biblical narratives such as the Exodus narrative

---

[64] Smith and Jayachitra, *Teaching All Nations*; Dube, "'Go Therefore and Make Disciples of All Nations' (Matt. 28:19a)," pp. 224–245; Soares-Prabhu, "Two Mission Commands," pp. 264–282.

[65] In recent years, much scholarly efforts have been made on the intersectional study of the Bible, race/ethnicity, and religion. Bailey, Liew, and Segovia, *They Were All Together in One Place?*; Brett, *Ethnicity and the Bible*; Buell, *Why This New Race*; Hockey and Horrell, *Ethnicity, Race, Religion*; Horrell and Lieu, *Ethnicity and Inclusion*; Nasrallah and Fiorenza, *Prejudice and Christian Beginnings*; Smith and Choi, *Minoritized Women Reading Race and Ethnicity*. See also Kim, "Race, Ethnicity and the Gospels."

[66] Concerning Ham, see Goldenberg, *Curse of Ham*; Haynes, *Noah's Curse*. Regarding Hagar, see Junior, *Reimagining Hagar*. See also Gafney, "Hagar." For womanist interpretation of the Bible, see Byron and Lovelace, *Womanist Interpretations of the Bible*.

[67] Byron and Lovelace, *Womanist Interpretations of the Bible*.

and Jesus's teaching have fostered social justice and race relations. In the following, we will see the landscape of contemporary biblical interpretations concerning race, ethnicity, and race relations.

4.1 Exodus, Liberation, and the Conquest Narrative in Joshua

The narrative of exodus is a prime example of biblical theology that emphasizes the importance of justice and freedom. The Hebrew slaves kept in Egypt were freed by God through the leadership of Moses. In the narrative, God heard their cries and cared for them. So much so that many people love this story of liberation and God's preferential option for the marginalized. Yet the issue is that this narrative of liberation continues with the conquest narrative in Joshua.[68] The thorny question is how to understand God's liberation of Israelites and his command to kill all the Canaanites. Is this the same God? Is this conflict in God's actions due to a different understanding of God? Traditionally, the solution has been either spiritualizing or allegorizing such a narrative or justifying it from the perspective of biblical theology. In the former, the biblical narrative applies to personal lives where one needs to obey God under any circumstances. Here, the teaching is that one should not fear any threats or obstacles because God will be leading the one who is courageous and faithful. In the latter, some people justify the conquest narrative from the point of biblical theology in that God destined such roads or fates for the Canaanites. But other scholars point out the Jewish ideology of conquest and control of others in the conquest narrative in Joshua.[69] As seen here, the issue is about interpretation. How can we interpret all triumphant biblical stories? In the same vein, we need to reengage Sarah and Hagar in the Genesis narrative. In the narrative, Sarah and Abraham take God on their side and expel Hagar and Ishmael. Is there a way to read Hagar's story differently from Jewish covenantal theology? If all biblical stories are perspectival, whose meaning can we take?[70]

4.2 Jesus Engaging a Canaanite Woman (Matthew 15:21–28)

Race or ethnicity is a complex element in the gospel stories because it comes with one's class or economic conditions. We will deal with two controversial narratives in the gospels: one in which Jesus is engaging a Canaanite woman (Matt 15:21–28), and the other, a Samaritan woman (John 4:1–42). Since we saw these stories in the previous section, here, the focus is to highlight different

---

[68] See Warrior, "Canaanites, Cowboys, and Indians," pp. 261–265.

[69] Warrior, "Canaanites, Cowboys, and Indians," pp. 261–265. See also Hawk, "The Truth about Conquest," pp. 129–140.

[70] Regarding Hagar, see Junior, *Reimagining Hagar*. See also Gafney, "Hagar." For womanist interpretation of the Bible, see Byron and Lovelace, *Womanist Interpretations of the Bible*.

scholarly interpretations of these stories. In Matt 15:21–28, Jesus is mean to the Canaanite woman. A similar story also appears in Mark 7:24–30, where a woman encounters a Syrophoenician (meaning, a gentile) woman. In both texts, the woman is a gentile, that is, she is more marginalized than a man. She is also a mother of a daughter. In these stories, it is impossible to separate race/ethnicity from her other conditions of gender and being a mother, not to mention her economic condition. In Matthew's story, however, her condition is aggravated since she is named a Canaanite woman, part of Israel's enemy for a long time. We can think of four possible scholarly approaches to this story of a Canaanite woman. First, traditional biblical theologians justify the harshness of Jesus's demeanor to this woman, saying that his intention is not to disparage her but to test her. Likewise, they say that calling her a dog is comic or friendly as if the dog was a pet. Here, Jesus is the same as God, who is almighty and saves people willingly. Her faith is then absolute obedience to Jesus. The implication is she does not care about Jesus's derogatory language; her faith says that she can do whatever if she gets what she wants. Also, the point is that race or ethnicity does not matter in this story because faith erases the distinctions of race or ethnicity. Anyone who comes to Jesus with absolute allegiance joins a people of God, based on allegiance. This kind of allegiance-based interpretation is reminiscent of covenantal theology in Sarah and Hagar. In other words, as God is not questioned in that theology, Jesus is intact in this story and acts like a god. But clearly, in this story of Matthew, Jesus appears as a Jewish Messiah who claims Jewish prerogatives and exclusive theology that gentiles are outside God's salvation (Matt 15:24–26). In the end, this Canaanite woman accepted such a view, satisfying herself with the healing of her daughter and making herself still a foreign woman.

Second, some scholars argue that Jesus changed his mind because of her challenge.[71] It is certainly possible that Jesus gradually changed his view of mission and theology toward others. As a Jew, he was comfortable with the traditional Jewish belief that they are a special people of God. But as the story goes on, Jesus realized that faith is more important than race or ethnicity. More importantly, here, her faith is not simply about Jesus but about God who must bless her and her daughter. Even though the Jewish messiah rejected her request a few times, she knew that the Messiah should have blessed her as well. Her faith says that God cares for others and that the Jewish messiah must do that work. So she was persistent until she was heard. This is the faith for which Jesus found and commended. In this interpretation, Jesus becomes a model of

---

[71] Schipani, "Transformation in the Borderlands," pp. 13–24; Patte, "The Canaanite Woman and Jesus," pp. 33–53.

discipleship. At the borderlands, he encounters a Canaanite woman; he experiences a transformation that faith is all that is required regardless of race or ethnicity.

Third, other scholars point out the "challenging faith" of this woman, and the focus is on her bold insistence that she is blessed and shares the table with Jewish children.[72] In her humorous yet persistent faith that her daughter needs healing, interpreters see the radical nature of her challenging faith. That is, she seeks justice, not merely healing. In this sense, she is a radical voice for justice, freedom, and equality.

Fourth, still other scholars interpret the story of the Canaanite woman from the perspective of Matthew's gospel or community, which struggles with mission strategy about gentiles.[73] As the community receives gentile members, some people question the validity of their inclusion. Or some of them wonder on what conditions they would need to accept gentiles into the church. This story of a Canaanite woman reflects that struggle in the community. In this story, Jesus represents two different mission strategies. On the one hand, Jesus and his disciples are united in rejecting her request (Matt 15:22–26). This means they represent the traditional Jewish perspective that God only cares for the Jews. But as the story unfolds, finally, in Matt 15:28, Jesus acknowledges her faith. At this point, Jesus reflects the revised mission strategy adopted by Matthew. That is, all, regardless of race, gender, or ethnicity, are included in the children of God through faith. Here, the point is that race/ethnicity is not unimportant, but it does not prevent one from accessing God's blessing. Therefore, ultimately, it is a matter of interpretation to what extent that gentiles are fully included in the community. Are they proud of their racial or ethnic identity or willing to forego their social and ethnic status?

4.3 Jesus Engaging a Samaritan Woman (John 4:1–42)

Concerning Jesus encountering a Samaritan woman in John 4:1–42, scholarly interpretations are also diverse.[74] First, the dominant Western interpretation

---

[72] Guardiola-Sáenz, "Borderless Women and Borderless Texts," pp. 69–81. See also Nadella, "The Motif of Hybridity in the Story of the Canaanite Woman and Its Relevance for Multi-faith Relations," pp. 111–120.

[73] Gullotta, "Among Dogs and Disciples," pp. 325–340; Klancher, *The Taming of the Canaanite Woman*; Levine, *The Social and Ethnic Dimensions of Matthean Social History.*

[74] On the one hand, some emphasize the Samaritan woman's active role in transforming her village and community. See, for example, Mukansengimana, Nyirimana, and Draper, "The Peacemaking Role of the Samaritan Woman in John 4:1–24," pp. 299–318. See also Okure, "Jesus and the Samaritan Woman (Jn 4:1–42) in Africa," pp. 401–418. On the other hand, others emphasize the problems of boundary/border crossing by Jesus from the postcolonial perspective. See Dube, "Reading for Decolonization (John 4:1–42)." See also Dube and Staley, *John and Postcolonialism.*

emphasizes both Jesus's superior position, as he is the divine Logos, and the woman's gradual, absolute faith in him. Jesus as the savior of the world engages this woman for his purpose that she and her people would accept him. He also goes beyond cultural or ethnic boundaries. This reading of John's Gospel includes high Christology that all peoples must accept Jesus as God. In other words, they are asked to abandon their previous lifestyle, culture, and religion. In this sense, the Samaritan woman plays a role in bringing her community to the larger community, that is, the people of God. They merge into a new people of God, abandoning their culture or ethnicity. But that is a myth because there is no such community devoid of race or ethnicity. Any community includes a notion of race, transcendent or not. Even when a new race of God is in view, that community is also a kind of race-conceived community. If any race of any kind takes center stage, other forms of living or ethnic identity may be degraded.

Second, interpreters may focus on the Samaritan woman's active engagement with Jesus.[75] In this case, the woman's positive relationship with Jesus and her active search for the truth are explored. It is her search for the truth that goes beyond her understanding. She changes her view of the Messiah and spreads the good news to her village people. In this interpretation, while her ethnic Samaritan identity is not abandoned, what is changed is her view of self and the Messiah. In the end, she becomes a transformative agent for her community such that her village people also find joy and freedom through the Messiah.

Third, postcolonial interpretation problematizes this story in John 4:1–42 for two reasons.[76] One is that the Johannine Gospel is entirely seen as a triumphant gospel that rejects other cultures and other narratives. The prologue in John is read this way that the word (*logos*) became Jesus, which means that Jesus, who was preexistent with God, came down to earth from heaven to deliver the people from sins. That is through accepting the word of Jesus or simply believing in him. Here, faith means accepting Jesus as the savior and the Lord. For example, the "I Am" sayings of Jesus are understood with high Christology-led salvation. When Jesus says that "I am the way, and the truth, and the life" in John 14:6, people understand that there are no other ways of salvation (John 14:6). The other reason is that readers interpret John's gospel in "exclusive" ways, based on high Christology and exclusivism, as we just saw in John 14:6. For the above two reasons, postcolonial interpretation points out the imperial voices of John's Gospel. If this is the case, other cultures and people are easily subjugated to the

---

[75] Mukansengimana, Nyirimana, and Draper, "The Peacemaking Role of the Samaritan Woman in John 4:1–24," pp. 299–318. See also Okure, "Jesus and the Samaritan Woman (Jn 4:1–42) in Africa," pp. 401–418.

[76] Dube, "Reading for Decolonization (John 4:1–42)"; Dube and Staley, *John and Postcolonialism*.

Western gospel, which considers faith as salvific knowledge and emphasizes forensic salvation, reminiscent of a legal court.

But John's Gospel is much more complex than the interpretations given previously. When we focus on the marginalized, the Johannine community's experience of separation and expulsion from the Jewish synagogue, the message of the "I Am" sayings of Jesus appears different.[77] That is the message of "I am the way" in John 14:6 may be a message of comfort and encouragement for them. Jesus's words serve as a canopy for the unstable community so that they may find themselves secure in a new place. Understood this way, John's Gospel is not a weapon to reject other cultures or invade other countries, rather it is a safe, comforting book for the Johannine community. It is not a triumphant gospel but an engaging gospel with which the marginalized people may find strength and hope. Furthermore, in my interpretation, the "I Am" sayings of Jesus can be understood as a description of Jesus's work.[78] That is, when Jesus says that "I am the way," it may mean his work of discerning God's nature. He exemplified the love of God in the world, risking his life, dying on the cross to reveal the way of God. He testified to the truth of God and did not fear Pilate (John 18:37). Because of his example, people can trust him and follow in his footsteps (John 8:31–32). A mere belief in him is not enough, as he says: "Then Jesus said to the Jews who had believed in him, 'If you continue in my word, you are truly my disciples; and you will know the truth, and the truth will make you free.'" If properly understood, John 14:6 may be an inviting space for intercultural engagement with other cultures or people since what Jesus asks is acting with love, testifying to the truth, and liberating life. His disciples are those who follow Jesus who loved God and the world so much.

4.4 Paul's Gospel and Race/Ethnicity

The Apostle Paul is a controversial figure, and his letters are hard to understand.[79] First, traditionally, he is seen as the champion of the gospel (*euangelion*) because he wrote about justification and faith (Rom 3:21–26; Gal 2:16–21). In this interpretation, the gospel is equated with "justification by faith," and it is opposed to the Jewish law, which is an impossible means of salvation. Jesus is the gospel because he died on the cross and dealt with sins. Those who accept Jesus's salvific death and have faith in him are justified once and for all as if they were in a legal court ("forensic salvation"). Then, there is no other way of salvation, as we saw in the traditional interpretation of John 14:6.

---

[77] Kim, *Truth, Testimony, and Transformation*, pp. 1–78. See also Smith and Kim, *Toward Decentering the New Testament*, pp. 161–175.

[78] Kim, *Truth, Testimony, and Transformation*, pp. 1–78.

[79] Kim, *How to Read Paul*, pp. 1–48.

In this traditional view, Paul's community is understood as a unified community in Christ, and likewise, "the body of Christ" in 1 Cor 12:27 is understood as a metaphorical organism.[80] The Corinthians, for instance, belong to a community, which is Christ's. Because they belong to the community, they must show allegiance to it. This view of community comes from Stoicism that emphasizes hierarchical unity in society. Because all people belong to society, as bodily parts belong to the body, they must work hard without complaining. In this thinking, there is no room for true diversity or equality or justice because of a rigid unity. Borrowing this Stoic idea of unity, many scholars have read Paul's body metaphor as placing Jesus Christ at the center of the community. Jesus Christ represents the central doctrine or teaching by the church. The hidden implication is that pastors are next to Christ, and other members are under them. Likewise, in this traditional understanding of Paul and his letters, he is considered a political conservative who adopts the social convention of gender and hierarchy. All thirteen letters traditionally attributed to him are considered his authentic letters. So slavery was warranted because of the household codes in the Deutero-Pauline and Pastoral Letters of which Pauline authorship is disputed (Col 3:18–4:1; Eph 5:21–6:9; Tit 2:1–10; cf, 1 Pet 2:18–3:7). Gender hierarchy was also granted because of these household codes. 1 Timothy 2:11–14 indicates women are subordinate to men. Ultimately, in this traditional view, Paul is a proponent of hierarchical unity where nontraditional thinking about Christ or non-Westerners hardly find and play their part.

Because of the previously mentioned traditional understanding of Paul, feminist, womanist, and postcolonial interpreters challenge the politically conservative version of Paul. They see him as an apocalyptic theologian and apostle who does not have an interest in social justice, gender equality, or global solidarity and peace. Partially, this claim seems true since he held an interim theology that soon the Lord comes back to judge the world. Because of this interim view, he did not directly confront or challenge social or political systems; rather, he wanted gradual personal transformations, as seen in Rom 12:1–2. That is certainly his limitation.

However, there is room for a better understanding of Paul not only because Paul's gospel has been largely misunderstood but also because Paul's body metaphor has been focused on unity alone.[81] Paul's gospel is not primarily about who is saved or how an individual is justified once and for all. The centerpiece

---

[80] Regarding a brief review of "the body of Christ," see Kim, *Christ's Body in Corinth*, pp. 11–31. See also Smith and Kim, *Toward Decentering the New Testament*, pp. 201–204. See also Kim, *How to Read Paul*, pp. 121–133.

[81] See Kim, *How to Read Paul*, pp. 49–62, 121–133; Kim, *Christ's Body in Corinth*, pp. 11–31. See also Smith and Kim, *Toward Decentering the New Testament*, pp. 201–204.

of his gospel is the salvation of all people and the inclusion of the gentiles into the people of God. As such, people may accept the love of God through the grace of Jesus. This is what faith means to Paul. Faith is trusting God and Jesus and showing faithfulness to God. Faith is not salvific knowledge but connotes one's faithful relationships with God and Jesus. Such faith is possible when one follows Jesus's faithfulness through which God's justice and love were manifested (Rom 3:22). While Paul's gospel is not a social-justice gospel, it is not the same as the Western gospel as we saw before. His vision is to spread the good news of God, which is the inclusion of the gentiles as well as Jews with faith. While his community is not a radical, revolutionary one due to his interim theology, it is not the same as the Stoic ideal of hierarchical unity. Rather, Paul's notion of community is a union where all distinctions come together and different people are united to Christ (Gal 3:28), who is the foundation of the community. This idea is not like the American melting pot theory where all distinctions of culture or ethnicity are erased. Here, union means a gathering of differences and different people who are connected to the spirit of Jesus and his faithfulness. In this understanding, there is room for diversity since each person holds his or her cultural identity. What is united with is not culture or forms of thought but Christ-like living. In this sense, 1 Cor 12:27 may be translated as "you are a Christic body, individually and communally," as I argued elsewhere.[82] This means that the Corinthian members must live ethically in response to Christ's faith, both individually and communally. So, here, "the body" is not a community as in a metaphorical organism but a way of life. Then, Gal 3:28 may be also understood differently with a focus on *Christic union* where all distinctions come together and support one another in Christ. Paul's saying in Gal 3:28 ("There is no longer Jew or Greek, there is no longer slave or free, there is no longer male and female; for all of you are one in Christ Jesus") is not primarily about social justice or equality, but it is about a Christ-like community where different people gather together in Christ and follow him. They are all accepted into the same community. Otherwise, their social status and ethnic identity remain unchanged until Parousia.

5 Conclusion

While inclusive monotheism in biblical traditions fosters race relations, exclusive monotheism is detrimental to them. While the former emphasizes God's love of all, the latter bifurcates people into two categories: those who are chosen and those who are not chosen. The example of exclusive monotheism is in

---

[82] See Kim, *How to Read Paul*, pp. 49–62, 121–133; Kim, *Christ's Body in Corinth*, pp. 11–31. See also Smith and Kim, *Toward Decentering the New Testament*, pp. 201–204.

Joshua's conquest narrative in which the Canaanites are seen as nobodies. But inclusive monotheism is widespread in biblical traditions. For example, the creation story and Abraham's call reflect God's love of all. God wants humanity to flourish by living in diversity. God calls Abraham, who is nobody, and gives him a new meaning of life. Abraham becomes the ancestor of all people who trust God. Jesus embraces the same God of Abraham, who "makes his sun rise on the evil and on the good, and sends rain on the righteous and on the unrighteous" (Matt 5:45). The Gospels are complex as they contain the Evangelists' theology, which involves race or ethnicity. While Matthew reflects Jewish exclusivism in the story of a Canaanite woman encountering Jesus, Luke embraces the salvation of the gentiles (Luke 4:16–30). John is also concerned with race/ethnicity in the story of a Samaritan woman encountering Jesus. Mark also contains stories of gentiles whom Jesus cares for. Overall, the Gospels foster race relations though there are complexities about how to interpret them. Apostle Paul and his letters are also very much concerned with race/ethnicity, as he wants to extend the gospel to all, including Jews.

Bibliography

Anderson, James S. *Monotheism and Yahweh's Appropriation of Baal.* New York, NY: T & T Clark, 2015.

Assmann, Jan. *The Price of Monotheism.* Trans. Robert Savage. Stanford, CA: Stanford University Press, 2010.

Bailey, Randall C., Tat-siong Benny Liew, and Fernando F. Segovia, eds. *They Were All Together in One Place? Toward Minority Biblical Criticism.* Semeia Studies. Atlanta, GA: Society of Biblical Literature, 2009.

Barnes, Michael. *In the Presence of Mystery: An Introduction to the Story of Human Religiousness.* Mystic, CT: Twenty-Third, 2003.

Bauckham, Richard. *God Crucified: Monotheism and Christology in the New Testament.* Grand Rapids, MI: Eerdmans, 1999.

Birch, Bruce et al. *A Theological Introduction to the Old Testament.* Nashville, TN: Abingdon, 2005.

Blount, Brian. *Go Preach! Mark's Kingdom Message and the Black Church Today.* Maryknoll, NY: Orbis, 1998.

Borg, Marcus and John Dominic Crossan. *The First Paul: Reclaiming the Radical Visionary Behind the Church's Conservative Icon.* New York: Harper Collins, 2009.

Brett, Mark, ed. *Ethnicity and the Bible.* Leiden: Brill, 1997.

Brueggemann, Walter. *An Introduction to the Old Testament: The Canon and Christian Imagination.* Louisville, KY: Westminster John Knox Press, 2003.

Buell, Denise Kimber. *Why This New Race: Ethnic Reasoning in Early Christianity.* New York: Columbia University Press, 2005.

Byron, Gay and Vanessa Lovelace, eds. *Womanist Interpretations of the Bible: Expanding the Discourse.* Semeia Studies. Atlanta, GA: Society of Biblical Literature, 2016.

Charlesworth, James. *The Historical Jesus: An Essential Guide.* Nashville, TN: Abingdon, 2008.

Collins, John. *A Short Introduction to the Hebrew Bible.* Minneapolis, MN: Fortress, 2007.

Coogan, Michael. *A Brief Introduction to the Old Testament: The Hebrew Bible in Its Context.* New York: Oxford University Press, 2012.

Crossan, Dominic. *The Historical Jesus: The Life of a Mediterranean Jewish Peasant.* San Francisco, CA: Harper Collins, 1991.

Crüsemann, Frank. *The Torah: Theology and Social History of Old Testament Law.* Minneapolis, MN: Fortress, 1996.

Culpepper, Alan. *The Gospel and Letters of John*. Nashville, TN: Abingdon, 1998.

De Vaux, Roland. *Ancient Israel: Its Life and Social Institutions*. New York: McGraw-Hill, 1965.

Dowd, Sharyn and Elizabeth Malbon. "The Significance of Jesus' Death in Mark: Narrative Context and Authorial Audience." *Journal of Biblical Literature* 125.2 (2006), pp. 271–297.

Dube, Musa W. "Reading for Decolonization (John 4:1–42)." *Semeia* 75 (1996), pp. 37–59.

———. "'Go Therefore and Make Disciples of All Nations' (Matt. 28:19a): A Postcolonial Perspective on Biblical Criticism and Pedagogy." In *Teaching the Bible*, ed. Fernando Segovia and Mary Ann Tolbert. Maryknoll, NY: Orbis Books, 1998, pp. 224–245.

Dube, Musa W. and Jeffrey Lloyd Staley, eds. *John and Postcolonialism: Travel, Space, and Power*. New York: Sheffield Academic Press, 2002.

Dunn, James. "Was Jesus a Monotheist?" In *Early Jewish and Christian Monotheism*, ed. Loren Stuckenbruck and Wendy Sproston North. New York: T & T Clark, 2004, pp. 104–119.

———. *Did the First Christians Worship Jesus? The New Testament Evidence*. Louisville, KY: Westminster John Knox Press, 2010.

Evans, Paul. "Imagining Justice for the Marginalized: A Suspicious Reading of the Covenant Code (Exodus 21:1–23:33) in Ancient Near Eastern Context." In *The Bible and Social Justice: Old Testament and New Testament Foundations for the Church's Urgent Call*, ed. Cynthia Long Westfall and Bryan R. Dyer. Eugene, OR: Pickwick, 2016, pp. 1–34.

Fletcher-Louis, Crispin. *Jesus Monotheism: Christological Origins: The Emerging Consensus and Beyond*. Eugene, OR: Cascade, 2015.

Frankfort, Henri. *Kingship and the Gods: A Study of Ancient Near Eastern Religion as the Integration of Society and Nature*. Chicago, IL: University of Chicago Press, 1948.

Gafney, Wil. "Hagar." *Bible Odyssey*. Accessed: June 9, 2021. www.bibleodyssey.org/en/people/main-articles/hagar.

Gnuse, Robert Karl. *No Other Gods: Emergent Monotheism in Israel*. Sheffield: Sheffield Academic Press, 1997.

Goldenberg, David M. *Curse of Ham: Race and Slavery in Early Judaism, Christianity, and Islam*. Princeton, NJ: Princeton University Press, 2003.

González, Justo L. *The Story Luke Tells: Luke's Unique Witness to the Gospel*. Grand Rapids, MI: Eerdmans, 2015.

Gottwald, Norman. *The Politics of Ancient Israel*. Library of Ancient Israel, ed. Douglas Knight. Louisville, KY: Westminster John Knox Press, 2001.

Guardiola-Sáenz, Leticia. "Borderless Women and Borderless Texts: A Cultural Reading of Matthew 15:21–28." *Semeia* 78 (1997), pp. 69–81.

Gullotta, Daniel N. "Among Dogs and Disciples: An Examination of the Story of the Canaanite Woman (Matthew 15:21–28) and the Question of the Gentile Mission within the Matthean Community." *Neotestamentica* 48.2 (2014), pp. 325–340.

Hawk, L. Daniel. "The Truth about Conquest: Joshua as History, Narrative, and Scripture." *Interpretation* 66.2 (2012), pp. 129–140.

Haynes, Stephen R. *Noah's Curse: The Biblical Justification of American Slavery.* Oxford: Oxford University Press, 2002.

Hays, Richard B. "PISTIS and Pauline Christology: What is at Stake?" In *Pauline Theology*, Vol. 4, ed. E. Elizabeth Johnson and David M. Hay. Atlanta, GA: Scholars Press, 1997, pp. 35–60.

The Faith of Jesus Christ: The Narrative Substructure of Galatians 3:1–4:11. Grand Rapids, MI: Eerdmans, 2002.

Hiebert, Theodore. "The Tower of Babel and the Origin of the World's Cultures." *Journal of Biblical Literature* 126 (2007), pp. 29–58.

Hillers, Delbert. Micah: A Commentary on the Book of the Prophet Micah. Philadelphia, PA: Fortress Press, 1984.

Hockey, Katherine M. and David G. Horrell, eds. *Ethnicity, Race, Religion: Identities and Ideologies in Early Jewish and Christian Texts, and in Modern Biblical Interpretation.* London: T&T Clark, 2019.

Horrell, David and Judith Lieu, eds. *Ethnicity and Inclusion: Religion, Race, and Whiteness in Constructions of Jewish and Christian Identities.* Grand Rapids, MI: Eerdmans, 2020.

Hurtado, Larry. *Honoring the Son: Jesus in Earliest Christian Devotional Practice.* Bellingham, WA: Lexham Press, 2018.

Johnson, Luke Timothy. "Rom 3:21–26 and the Faith of Jesus." *Catholic Biblical Quarterly* 44.1 (1982), pp. 77–90.

Junior, Nyasha. *Reimagining Hagar: Blackness and Bible.* Oxford: Oxford University Press, 2019.

Kim, Yung Suk. "Lex Talionis in Exod 21:22–25: Its Origin and Context." *Journal of Hebrew Scriptures* 3(2006), Article 3.

"Imitators (Mimetai) in 1 Cor 4:16 and 11:1: A New Reading of Threefold Embodiment." *Horizons in Biblical Theology* 33.2 (2011), pp. 147–170.

A Theological Introduction to Paul's Letters: Exploring a Threefold Theology of Paul. Eugene, OR: Cascade, 2011.

"Reclaiming Christ's Body (soma christou): Embodiment of God's Gospel in Paul's Letters." *Interpretation* 67.1 (2013), pp. 20–29.

Truth, Testimony, and Transformation: A New Reading of the "I Am" Sayings of Jesus in the Fourth Gospel. Eugene, OR: Cascade, 2014.

Resurrecting Jesus: The Renewal of New Testament Theology. Eugene, OR: Cascade, 2015.

Preaching the New Testament Again: Faith, Freedom, and Transformation. Eugene, OR: Cascade, 2019.

Rereading Galatians from the Perspective of Paul's Gospel: A Literary and Theological Commentary. Eugene, OR: Cascade, 2019.

Rereading Romans from the Perspective of Paul's Gospel: A Literary and Theological Commentary. Eugene, OR: Resource, 2019.

How to Read Paul: A Brief Introduction to His Theology, Writings, and World. Minneapolis, MN: Fortress, 2021.

"Race, Ethnicity and the Gospels." In *Oxford Bibliographies in Biblical Studies*, ed. Christopher Matthews. New York: Oxford University Press,2021.

Klancher, Nancy. *The Taming of the Canaanite Woman: Constructions of a Christian Identity in the Afterlife of Matthew 15:21–28.* Boston, MA: De Gruyter, 2013.

Knight, Douglas. "The Ethics of Human Life in the Hebrew Bible." In *Justice and the Holy: Essays in Honor of Walter Harrelson*, ed. Douglas A. Knight and Peter J. Paris. Atlanta, GA: Scholars Press, 1989, pp. 65–88.

Koch, Klaus. *The Prophets: The Assyrian Period.* Philadelphia, PA: Fortress, 1983.

Kristeva, Julia. *Strangers to Ourselves.* Trans. Leon S. Roudiez. New York: Columbia University Press, 1991.

Lee, Michelle. *Paul, the Stoics, and the Body of Christ.* Cambridge: Cambridge University Press, 2006.

Levine, Amy-Jill. *The Social and Ethnic Dimensions of Matthean Social History.* New York: Edwin Mellen, 1988.

Martin, Dale. *The Corinthian Body.* New Haven, CT: Yale University Press, 1995.

Martyn, J. Louis. *History and Theology in the Fourth Gospel.* Louisville, KY: Westminster John Knox Press, 2003.

McNutt, Paula. *Reconstructing the Society of Ancient Israel.* Library of Ancient Israel, ed. Douglas Knight. Louisville, KY: Westminster John Knox Press, 1999.

Mitchell, Margaret. *Paul's Rhetoric of Reconciliation.* Louisville, KY: Westminster John Knox Press, 1987.

Muilenburg, James. "Abraham and the Nations: Blessing and World History." *Interpretation* 19.4 (1965), pp. 387–398.

Mukansengimana, Rose Nyirimana and Jonathan Draper. "The Peacemaking Role of the Samaritan Woman in John 4:1–24: A Mirror and Challenge to Rwandan women." *Neotestamentica* 46.2 (2012), pp. 299–318.

Nadella, Raj. "The Motif of Hybridity in the Story of the Canaanite Woman and Its Relevance for Multi-faith Relations." In *Many Yet One? Multiple Religious Belonging*, ed. Peniel Jesudason Rufus Rajkumar and Joseph Prabhakar Dayam. Geneva: World Council of Churches, 2015, pp. 111–120.

Nasrallah, Laura and Elisabeth Schüssler Fiorenza, eds. *Prejudice and Christian Beginnings: Investigating Race, Gender, and Ethnicity in Early Christianity*. Minneapolis, MN: Fortress, 2009.

Neyrey, Jerome. *Paul in Other Worlds: A Cultural Reading of His Letter*. Louisville, KY: Westminster John Knox Press, 1990.

Norton, Yolanda. "Silenced Struggles for Survival: Finding Life in Death in the Book of Ruth." In *I Found God in Me: A Womanist Biblical Hermeneutics Reader*, ed. Mitzi J. Smith. Eugene, OR: Cascade, 2015, pp. 265–279.

Okure, Teresa. "Jesus and the Samaritan Woman (Jn 4:1–42) in Africa." *Theological Studies* 70.2 (2009), pp. 401–418.

Patte, Daniel. "The Canaanite Woman and Jesus: Surprising Models of Discipleship (Matt. 15:21–28)." In *Transformative Encounters*, ed. Ingrid Rosa Kitzberger. Atlanta, GA: Society of Biblical Literature, 2000, pp. 33–53.

"Reading Matthew 28:16–20 with Others: How Does It Deconstruct Our Western Concept of Mission?" *Hervormde Teologiese Studies* 62.2 (2006), pp. 521–557. www.researchgate.net/publication/45681165_Reading_Matthew_2816-20_with_Others_How_it_deconstructs_our_Western_concept_of_mission.

Paul, Shalom. *Amos: A Commentary of the Book of Amos*. Minneapolis, MN: Fortress, 1991.

Powell, Mark Alan. *Fortress Introduction to the Gospels*. Minneapolis, MN: Fortress, 2019.

Price, James L. "God's Righteousness Shall Prevail." *Interpretation* 28.3 (1974), pp. 259–280.

Roetzel, Calvin. *Paul: A Jew on the Margins*. Louisville, KY: Westminster John Knox Press, 2003.

Sanders, Ed Parish. *Paul and Palestinian Judaism*. Philadelphia, PA: Fortress, 1977.

Schipani, Daniel. "Transformation in the Borderlands." *Beginning of Life* 4.1 (2003), pp. 13–24.

Schwartz, Regina. *The Curse of Cain: The Violent Legacy of Monotheism*. Chicago, IL: University of Chicago Press, 1997.

Smith, Mark A. *The Origins of Biblical Monotheism: Israel's Polytheistic Background and the Ugaritic Texts*. New York: Oxford University Press, 2003.

Smith, Mitzi J. and Jin Young Choi, eds. *Minoritized Women Reading Race and Ethnicity: Intersectional Approaches to Constructed Identity and Early Christian (Con)Texts*. Lanham, MD: Lexington, 2020.

Smith, Mitzi J. and Lalitha Jayachitra, eds. *Teaching All Nations: Interrogating the Matthean Great Commission*. Minneapolis, MN: Fortress, 2014.

Smith, Mitzi J. and Yung Suk Kim. *Toward Decentering the New Testament: A Reintroduction*. Eugene, OR: Cascade, 2018.

Soares-Prabhu, George. "Two Mission Commands: An Interpretation of Matthew 28:16–20 in the Light of a Buddhist Text." *Biblical Interpretation* 2.4 (1994), pp. 264–282.

Sommer, Benjamin. *The Bodies of God and the World of Ancient Israel*. New York: Cambridge University Press, 2009.

"Monotheism in the Hebrew Bible." *Bible Odyssey*. Accessed: June 8, 2021. www.bibleodyssey.org/en/people/related-articles/monotheism-in-the-hebrew-bible.

Stanley, Christopher. *The Hebrew Bible: A Comparative Approach*. Minneapolis, MN: Fortress, 2010.

Stanton, Graham. *The Gospels and Jesus*. Oxford: Oxford University Press, 2002.

Stendahl, Krister. "The Apostle Paul and the Introspective Conscience of the West." *Harvard Theological Review* 56.3 (1963), pp. 199–215.

"Religious Pluralism and the Claim to Uniqueness." In *Education as Transformation: Religious Pluralism, Spirituality, and a New Vision for Higher Education in America*, ed. Victor Kazanjian Jr and Peter Laurence. New York: Peter Lang, 2000, pp. 181–183.

Sussman, Robert. *The Myth of Race: The Troubling Persistence of an Unscientific Idea*. Cambridge, MA: Harvard University Press, 2014.

Talmon, Shemaryahu. *King, Cult and Calendar in Ancient Israel: Collected Studies*. Jerusalem: Magnes, 1986.

Van Seters, John. "Comparison of Babylonian Codes with the Covenant Code and Its Implications for the Study of Hebrew Law." Unpublished paper delvered at Society of Biblical Literature Annual Meetings 2001.

Von Rad, Gerhard. *Genesis: A Commentary*. Louisville, KY: Westminster John Knox Press, 1973.

Wafawanaka, Robert. *Am I Still My Brother's Keeper? Biblical Perspectives on Poverty*. Lanham, MD: University Press of America, 2012.

Warrior, Robert. "Canaanites, Cowboys, and Indians: Deliverance, Conquest, and Liberation Theology Today." *Christianity and Crisis* 49 (1989–1990), pp. 261–265. Reprinted in *Native and Christian: Indigenous Voices on*

Religious Identity in the United States and Canada, ed. James Treat. New York: Routledge, 1996.

Whitelam, Keith. "Israelite Kingship: The Royal Ideology and Its Opponents." In *The World of Ancient Israel*, ed. Ronald E. Clements. Cambridge: Cambridge University Press, 1989, pp. 119–139.

Yee, Gale. "'She Stood in Tears amid the Alien Corn': Ruth, the Perpetual Foreigner and Model Minority." In *They Were All Together in One Place? Toward Minority Biblical Criticism*, ed. Randall C. Bailey, Tat-Siong Benny Liew, and Fernando F. Segovia. Atlanta, GA: Society of Biblical Literature, 2009, pp. 119–140.

Cambridge Elements ☰

Religion and Monotheism

Paul K. Moser
Loyola University Chicago

Paul K. Moser is a professor of philosophy at Loyola University Chicago. He is the author of *Understanding Religious Experience, The God Relationship, The Elusive God* (winner of national book award from the Jesuit Honor Society), *The Evidence for God, The Severity of God; Knowledge and Evidence (*all Cambridge University Press), and *Philosophy after Objectivity* (Oxford University Press); co-author of *Theory of Knowledge* (Oxford University Press); editor of *Jesus and Philosophy* (Cambridge University Press) and *The Oxford Handbook of Epistemology* (Oxford University Press); and co-editor of *The Wisdom of the Christian Faith (*Cambridge University Press). He is the co-editor with Chad Meister of the book series *Cambridge Studies in Religion, Philosophy, and Society.*

Chad Meister
Bethel University

Chad Meister is a professor of philosophy and theology and department chair at Bethel College. He is the author of *Introducing Philosophy of Religion* (Routledge, 2009), *Christian Thought: A Historical Introduction*, 2nd edition (Routledge, 2017), and *Evil: A Guide for the Perplexed*, 2nd edition (Bloomsbury, 2018). He has edited or co-edited the following: *The Oxford Handbook of Religious Diversity* (Oxford University Press, 2010); *Debating Christian Theism* (Oxford University Press, 2011), with Paul Moser; *The Cambridge Companion to the Problem of Evil* (Cambridge University Press, 2017); and with Charles Taliaferro, *The History of Evil* (Routledge 2018, in six volumes).

About the Series

This Cambridge Element series publishes original concise volumes on monotheism and its significance. Monotheism as occupied inquirers since the time of the Biblical patriarch, and it continues to attract interdisciplinary academic work today. Engaging, current, and concise, the Elements benefit teachers, researched, and advanced students in religious studies, Biblical studies, theology, philosophy of religion, and related fields.

Cambridge Elements ☰

Religion and Monotheism

Elements in the series

A full series listing is available at: www.cambridge.org/er&m